ALDOUS HUXLEY

*

Proper Studies

By ALDOUS HUXLEY

Novels
CROME YELLOW *
ANTIC HAY *
THOSE BARREN LEAVES *
POINT COUNTER POINT *
BRAVE NEW WORLD *
EYELESS IN GAZA *
AFTER MANY A SUMMER *
TIME MUST HAVE A STOP
APE AND ESSENCE

Short Stories
LIMBO *
MORTAL COILS *
LITTLE MEXICAN *
TWO OR THREE GRACES *
BRIEF CANDLES *

Biography
GREY EMINENCE

Essays and Belles Lettres
ON THE MARGIN *
ALONG THE ROAD *
PROPER STUDIES *
DO WHAT YOU WILL *
MUSIC AT NIGHT & *
VULGARITY IN LITERATURE
TEXTS AND PRETEXTS (Anthology) *
THE OLIVE TREE *
ENDS AND MEANS (An Enquiry
into the Nature of Ideals) *
THE ART OF SEEING
THE PERENNIAL PHILOSOPHY
SCIENCE, LIBERTY AND PEACE

Travel
JESTING PILATE (Illustrated) *
BEYOND THE MEXIQUE BAY (Illustrated) *

Poetry and Drama
VERSES AND A COMEDY *
(including early poems, Leda, The Cicadas
and The World of Light, a Comedy)
THE GIOCONDA SMILE

* Issued in this Collected Edition

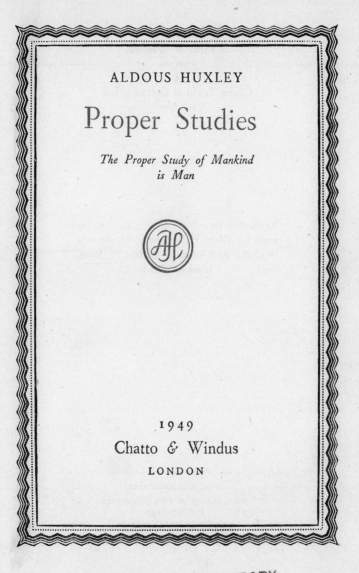

ALDOUS HUXLEY

Proper Studies

*The Proper Study of Mankind
is Man*

1949

Chatto & Windus

LONDON

PUBLISHED BY

Chatto & Windus

LONDON

*

Clarke, Irwin & Company Ltd

TORONTO

Applications regarding translation rights in any
work by Aldous Huxley should be addressed
to Chatto & Windus, 40 William IV Street,
London, W.C. 2

FIRST PUBLISHED 1927
FIRST ISSUED IN THIS COLLECTED
EDITION 1949
PRINTED IN GREAT BRITAIN

CONTENTS

INTRODUCTION

MEASURABLE AND UNMEASURABLE

Atoms, or perhaps it would be more accurate to say those aspects of the atom which scientists choose to consider, are immeasurably less complicated than men. And yet nobody who is not professionally a physicist would venture to discuss the nature of atoms. Where man is concerned, the case is different. Not only the professional anthropologist or sociologist, but every human being thinks himself qualified, by the mere fact of his humanity, to lay down the law about man and society—and with what arrogance, too often, what absurd cocksureness ! An amateur like the rest, I too rush in. But before rushing, I would offer some brief apology and explanation.

The atom of the scientists is simple in comparison with man in his totality. Its very simplicity is what renders its study by the layman so difficult. For the atom that science has chosen to study is a measurable abstraction from the real atom. It follows, therefore, that it can be studied only by those who have learned the technique of measurement—by those, that is to say, who are familiar with mathematics and the arts of experimentation.

Man also has his purely measurable aspects,

and to understand them one must be something of a physiologist, a bio-chemist, a geneticist ; something of a statistician and an economist ; of an educationist and a laboratory psychologist. But when all that is at present measurable in man has been duly measured, there remains a vast domain that cannot be accurately explored with the surveying instruments of physical science. For the purposes of practical living, this yet unmeasured and perhaps for ever unmeasurable domain is of supreme importance. Man in his totality comprises the measurable as well as the unmeasured aspects of his being, and no account of him can be complete which does not comprehend the results of scientific measurement and relate them intelligibly to that which is unmeasured. But though incomplete, an account of man exclusively in terms of his unmeasured characteristics can be of the highest utility. One can be a sage without being an actuary or a geneticist ; one can know oneself and the, humanly speaking, most important things about other people without knowing a word of bio-chemistry or the rudiments of scientific psychology. Herein lies the amateur's excuse. The most important part of man can be studied without a special technique, and described in the language of common speech. In order to be able to say something significant about man, one does not need to have had a special training. Indeed, some of the most significant things have been said by men who had no regular education of any kind.

I make no claim to be one of these natural sages, these born intuitive knowers of human nature. Nor can I pretend to be a professional in the arts of measuring what can be measured. Such modest talents, as psychologist and observer, as I possess are supplemented only by the sketchy training of the interested amateur. These essays represent an attempt on my part to methodize the confused notions, which I have derived from observation and reading, about a few of the more important aspects of social and individual life. It is my hope that in the process of clarifying my own thoughts I may help to clarify the thoughts of those who accompany me through these studies.

THE ORGANIZERS AND THE UTOPIANS

Sociological writings are too often either merely technical and practical, or else merely Utopian. The technicians do good work in criticizing current methods of social organization and suggesting detailed improvements. But like all organizers, they are apt, in the midst of administrative technicalities, to forget what it is they are organizing ; like all critics of detail, they are inclined to accept too complacently the main framework of the structure whose details they are trying to improve. They are no Utopians, brooding on things as they ought to be but are not. They accept things as they are, but too uncritically ; for along with the existing social institutions they accept that conception of human nature which the institutions imply.

The Utopians, on the other hand, accept nothing. They are too much preoccupied with what ought to be to pay any serious attention to what is. Outward reality disgusts them ; the compensatory dream is the universe in which they live. The subject of their meditations is not man, but a monster of rationality and virtue — of one kind of rationality and virtue at that, their own. The inhabitants of Utopia are radically unlike human beings. Their creators spend all their ink and energy in discussing, not what actually happens, but what would happen if men and women were quite different from what they are and from what, throughout recorded history, they have always been. It is as though astronomers wrote books about what would happen if there were no such thing as gravitation and if the earth, in consequence, moved in a straight line and not in an ellipse. Such books might be very edifying, if their authors began by showing that movement in a straight line is better than movement in a curve. (This, it may be remarked, they can do very easily ; they have only to call a straight line by its old-fashioned name, a 'right line,' and the trick is done. In precisely the same way—by using a word with a double meaning—Aristotle proved that the circle was the 'perfect' figure.) Such books, I repeat, might be edifying ; but they would not be of much help to any one desirous of studying celestial mechanics. Similarly, descriptions of Utopian worlds, where human nature is different from human nature in this world, may possibly be comforting and uplifting, may even stimulate their readers to revolutionary action ; but to the would-be sociologist, to the judicious reformer, who wants to know what direction reform should take and what are its limits, they have little or nothing to say.

FROM HUMAN NATURE TO SOCIAL INSTITUTIONS

Unqualified by training to discuss the details of existing social organization, by nature uninterested in hypothetical Utopias, I have tried to steer a middle course between the too immediate and concrete on the one hand and the too vague and remote on the other. I have tried to give an account, in the most general terms, and in regard to only a few selected aspects of life, of what is. In the light of what is and of what, therefore, might be, I have tried in certain cases to show what ought to be. To be more specific, I have studied first of all certain aspects of individual human nature, and having reached certain conclusions about the individual, I have gone on to consider existing and possible future institutions in the light of those conclusions. Social institutions exist for man, not man for social institutions. The only social institutions which will work for any length of time are those which are in harmony with individual human nature. Institutions which deny the facts of human nature either break down more or less violently, or else decay gradually into ineffectiveness. A knowledge of human nature provides us with a standard by which to judge existing institutions and all proposals for their reform. Given the individual, we are able to deduce the desirable institution.

The political philosophers of the eighteenth century employed this method in all their sociological speculations. From the postulate of individual human nature they deduced a whole army of logically necessary conclusions about institutions actually existing, or possible and desirable. Many of the conclusions at which they then arrived have since been acted upon. Our present institutions are to a great extent the institutions imagined by the eighteenth-century philosophers, using the method which I propose to follow in these essays. This is a fact which should make us extremely suspicious of the method. Contemporary institutions are not so perfect that we can blindly accept as valid the system of thought whose practical results they are. But when, put on our guard by the spectacle of the world around us, we examine the work of the eighteenth-century philosophers, we discover that where they went astray was not in using the method which deduces institutions from human nature (the method, it seems to me, is proof against all objections) ; it was in adopting an entirely false conception of individual human nature. The logic by which they deduced institutions was faultless ; given their view of human nature, the conclusions at which they arrived were necessary conclusions. But since their view of human nature was false, these necessary conclusions were also necessarily false. The better the logic, the more necessary the falsity of conclusions drawn from false premisses.

PSYCHOLOGIES OLD AND NEW

The curious thing about eighteenth-century psychology is that its falsity was gratuitous and novel. The working psychology of preceding epochs—the psychology, that is to say, elaborated through ages of experience by the Catholic Church—was eminently realistic. The men of the eighteenth century invented (or rather deduced, by a process which I shall describe in a subsequent essay, from existing metaphysical postulates) a new and fantastic psychology, which they could only reconcile with the observable facts by means of a specially contrived casuistry. Our democratic social institutions have been evolved in order to fit the entirely fabulous human nature of the eighteenth-century philosophers. Thanks partly to the inevitable failure of these institutions to produce the anticipated results, we have ceased to believe in that psychology. The modern conception of human nature is far closer to the traditional Catholic conception than to that of Helvétius or Godwin, Babeuf or Shelley. Starting from this much more realistic psychology of the individual, we can repeat the process by which the eighteenth-century philosophers deduced institutions from human nature. Our premisses being, I will not say true, but in any case vastly less faulty than theirs, it follows that our conclusions must be sounder. The institutions which fit our human nature cannot fail to work better than those which fitted the fantastic human nature of Helvétius and Rousseau.

So much for the method employed in these essays. All my criticisms of existing institutions, all my speculations about possible and desirable institutions, are based on the studies of individual human nature with which the book begins. The essays contained in this volume are separate and unconnected studies of a few aspects of human life. They make no claim to constitute a coherent system. The most that can be said for them is that, though unconnected, they are all situated, so to speak, at points on the outline of a possible system.

CAUSES

Sociologists and historians are inclined to talk altogether too glibly about the 'causes' of events, thoughts, and actions in the human universe. Now the human universe is so enormously complicated that to speak of *the* cause of any event is an absurdity. The causes of even the simplest event are very numerous, and any one who would discover even a few of them must take into consideration, among other things, the race to which the men and women participating in it belonged, the physiological state of the principal actors, their innate psychological peculiarities, and the tradition, the education, the environment which modified, restrained, and gave direction to their instincts, impulses, and thoughts. After having exhausted all the strictly human origins of events, the enthusiast for causes would have to consider the share taken by its non-human antecedents and accompaniments in bringing it about— the share taken by matter on the one hand and by such spiritual or metaphysical entities on the other as the seeker for causes may care to postulate. The facts of history have been explained in terms of the will of God, of the class war, of moral law, of climate, of the caprices and physiological peculiarities of those in power, of economic struggle, of race, of pure reason making judicious choice of the pleasurable, of blind animal instinct. You pay your money and you take your choice of a social and historical philosophy. Now it is obvious that the quality of the event changes completely according to the cause you choose to give it. Historical facts are qualitatively functions of the causes to which they are attributed. For example, a revolution caused by economic forces is not identical with the same revolution caused by the chronic indigestion of a king, or the will of a revengeful and outraged deity. An outburst of artistic activity caused (as the Freudians would have us believe) by a sudden happy efflorescence of sexual perversity is not identical with the same renascence caused by the stimulating and liberating action on the spirit of a multiplicity of inventions, discoveries, economic changes and political upheavals. Historians and sociologists who set out with preconceived ideas about the causes of events distort the facts by attributing them to causes of one particular kind, to the exclusion of all others. Now it is obvious that, in the nature of things, no human being can possibly know all the causes of any event. (And *anyhow*, as the Americans would say, what is a cause ?) The best that any observer can do is to present the facts, and with them a few of the most humanly significant antecedents and accompaniments which seem to be invariably connected with facts of that particular class. He will make it clear that the antecedents and accompaniments he has chosen for exposition are not the sole and exclusive causes of the facts, which he will describe, so to say, neutrally and without prejudging them, so that it will always be possible, without changing the quality of the facts, to add fresh causes to the list of determining correlations as they are discovered. I do not pretend to have achieved this difficult and perhaps humanly impossible neutrality. I have attributed causes with too much facility, and as though they were the exclusive determinants of the facts in question. In doing this I have prejudged the quality of the facts, and thereby, no doubt, distorted the total picture of them. The process is doubtless inevitable. For the powers of every mind are strictly limited ; we have our inborn idiosyncrasies, our acquired sentiments, prejudices, scales of value ; it is impossible for any man to transcend himself. Being what I am, I attribute one kind of causes to facts, and thereby distort them in one direction ; another man with a different mind and different upbringing would attribute other causes, and so distort the same facts in another way. The best I can do is to warn the reader against my distortion of the facts, and invite him to correct it by means of his own.

The author to whom I owe the most is the Italian, Vilfredo Pareto. In his monumental *Sociologia Generale* I discovered many of my own still vague and inchoate notions methodically set down and learnedly documented, together with a host of new ideas and relevant facts. I have borrowed freely from this almost inexhaustible store. Pareto's book does not make easy reading ; there are two thousand pages of it, to begin with. The matter is densely concentrated, and the dulness of the algebraical manner is only relieved by occasional flashes—if flashes be the right word to describe anything so slow, subfusc, and grim—of a humour that combines professorial heaviness with an almost mediaeval ferocity. It is, however, a superb piece of work, which deserves to be better known than it seems to be, at any rate in England. I shall be well satisfied if I succeed in introducing Pareto to a few new readers.

Another very remarkable and too little known book, to which I owe a great debt, is Professor L. Rougier's *Paralogismes du Rationalisme*. Professor Rougier is a mathematician, a philosopher, and a scholar profoundly learned in the history of thought. His book is a model of lucid analysis and elegant composition.

Less clear, less Frenchly coherent, are the writings of Georges Sorel. But the profundity and importance of what the author of *Reflexions sur la Violence* has to say make up for any oracular obscurity in his manner of saying.

Other sociological writers whom I have read with profit are Professor Graham Wallas and Mr. H. G. Wells, Dr. Trotter, Dr. Harvey Robinson, and M. Lévy-Bruhl.

Among the psychologists who have been of assistance to me, I must give a high place to Cardinal Newman, whose analysis of the psychology of thought remains one of the most acute, as it is certainly the most elegant, which has ever been made. Of contemporary psychologists, Jung strikes me as being by far the most highly gifted. His books on psychological types and on the unconscious are works of cardinal importance. By comparison with Jung, most other psychologists seem either uninspired, unilluminating, and soundly dull, or else, like Freud and Adler, monomaniacal.

PROPER STUDIES

THE IDEA OF EQUALITY

SUNDAY FAITH AND WEEKDAY FAITH

That all men are equal is a proposition to which, at ordinary times, no sane human being has ever given his assent. A man who has to undergo a dangerous operation does not act on the assumption that one doctor is just as good as another. Editors do not print every contribution that reaches them. And when they require Civil Servants, even the most democratic governments make a careful selection among their theoretically equal subjects. At ordinary times, then, we are perfectly certain that men are not equal. But when, in a democratic country, we think or act politically we are no less certain that men are equal. Or at any rate—which comes to the same thing in practice—we behave as though we were certain of men's equality. Similarly, the pious mediaeval nobleman who, in church, believed in forgiving enemies and turning the other cheek, was ready, as soon as he had emerged again into the light of day, to draw his sword at the slightest provocation. The human mind has an almost infinite capacity for being inconsistent.

The amount of time during which men are engaged in thinking or acting politically is very small when compared with the whole period of their lives ; but the brief activities of man the politician exercise a disproportionate influence on the daily life of man the worker, man at play, man the father and husband, man the owner of property. Hence the importance of knowing what he thinks in his political capacity and why he thinks it.

THE EQUALITARIAN AXIOM

Politicians and political philosophers have often talked about the equality of man as though it were a necessary and unavoidable idea, an idea which human beings must believe in, just as they must, from the very nature of their physical and mental constitution, believe in such notions as weight, heat, and light. Man is 'by nature free, equal, and independent,' says Locke, with the calm assurance of one who knows he is saying something that cannot be contradicted. It would be possible to quote literally thousands of similar pronouncements. One must be mad, says Babeuf, to deny so manifest a truth.

EQUALITY AND CHRISTIANITY

In point of historical fact, however, the notion of human equality is of recent growth, and so far from being a directly apprehended and necessary truth, is a conclusion logically drawn from pre-existing metaphysical assumptions. In modern times the Christian doctrines of the brotherhood of men and of their equality before God have been invoked in support of political democracy. Quite illogically, however. For the brotherhood of men does not imply their equality. Families have their fools and their men of genius, their black sheep and their saints, their worldly successes and their worldly failures. A man should treat his brothers lovingly and with justice, according to the deserts of each. But the deserts of every brother are not the same. Neither does men's equality before God imply their equality as among themselves. Compared with an infinite quantity, all finite quantities may be regarded as equal. There is no difference, where infinity is concerned, between one and a thousand. But leave infinity out of the question, and a thousand is very different from one. Our world is a world of finite quantities, and where worldly matters are concerned, the fact that all men are equal in relation to the infinite quantity which is God, is entirely irrelevant. The Church has at all times conducted its worldly policy on the assumption that it was irrelevant. It is only recently that the theorists of democracy have appealed to Christian doctrine for a confirmation of their equalitarian principles. Christian doctrine, as I have shown, gives no such support.

EQUALITY AND THE PHILOSOPHER

The writers who in the course of the eighteenth century supplied our modern political democracy with its philosophical basis did not turn to Christianity to find the doctrine of human equality. They were, to begin with, almost without exception anti-clerical writers, to whom the idea of accepting any assistance from the Church would have been extremely repugnant. Moreover, the Church, as organized for its worldly activities, offered them no assistance, but a frank hostility. It represented, even more clearly than the monarchical and feudal state, that mediaeval principle of hierarchical, aristocratic government against which, precisely, the equalitarians were protesting.

The origin of our modern idea of human equality is to be found in the philosophy of Aristotle. The tutor of Alexander the Great was not, it is true, a democrat. Living as he did in a slave-holding society, he regarded slavery as a necessary state of affairs. Whatever is, is right ; the familiar is the reasonable ; and Aristotle was an owner of slaves, not a slave himself ; he had no cause to complain. In his political philosophy he rationalized his satisfaction with the existing state of things, and affirmed that some men are born to be masters (himself, it went without saying, among them) and others to be slaves. But in saying this he was committing an inconsistency. For it was a fundamental tenet of his metaphysical system that specific qualities are the same in every member of a species. Individuals of one species are the same in essence or substance. Two human beings differ from one another in matter, but are the same in essence, as being both rational animals. The essential human quality which distinguishes the species Man from all other species is identical in both.

INCONSISTENCIES

How are we to reconcile this doctrine with Aristotle's statement that some men are born to be masters and others slaves ? Clearly, no reconciliation is possible ; the doctrines are contradictory. Aristotle said one thing when he was discussing the abstract problems of metaphysics and another when, as a slave-owner, he was discussing politics. Such inconsistencies are extremely common, and are generally made in perfectly good faith. In cases where material interests are at stake, where social and religious traditions, inculcated in childhood, and consequently incorporated into the very structure of the mind, can exercise their influence, men will naturally think in one way ; in other cases, where their interests and their early-acquired beliefs are not concerned, they will as naturally and inevitably think in quite a different way. A man who thinks and behaves as an open-minded unprejudiced scientist so long as he is repairing his automobile, will be outraged if asked to think about the creation of the world or the future life except in terms of the mythology current among the barbarous Semites three thousand years ago ; and though quite ready to admit that the present system of wireless telephony might be improved, he will regard any one who desires to alter the existing economic and political system as either a madman or a criminal. The greatest men of genius have not been exempt from these curious inconsistencies. Newton created the science of celestial mechanics ; but he was also the author of *Observations on the Prophecies of Daniel and the Apocalypse of St. John,* of a *Lexicon Propheticum* and a *History of the Creation.* With one part of his mind he believed in the miracles and prophecies about which he had been taught in childhood ; with another part he believed that the universe is a scene of order and uniformity. The two parts were impenetrably divided one from the other. The mathematical physicist never interfered with the commentator on the Apocalypse ; the believer in miracles had no share in formulating the laws of gravitation. Similarly, Aristotle the slave-owner believed that some men are born to command and others to serve ; Aristotle the metaphysician, thinking in the abstract, and unaffected by the social prejudices which influenced the slave-owner, expounded a doctrine of specific essences, which entailed belief in the real and substantial equality of all human beings. The opinion of the slave-

owner was probably nearer the truth than that
of the metaphysician. But it is by the metaphysician's doctrine that our lives are influenced
to-day.

APPLIED METAPHYSICS

That all the members of a species are identical
in essence was still, in the Middle Ages, a purely
metaphysical doctrine. No attempt was made
to apply it practically in politics. So long as the
feudal and ecclesiastical hierarchies served their
purpose of government, they seemed, to all but
a very few, necessary and unquestionable. Whatever is, is right ; feudalism and Catholicism *were*.
It was only after what we call the Reformation
and the Renaissance, when, under the stress of
new economic and intellectual forces, the old
system had largely broken down, that men began
to think of applying the metaphysical doctrine
of Aristotle and his mediaeval disciples to politics.
Feudalism and ecclesiastical authority lingered
on, but as the merest ghosts of themselves. They
had, to all intents and purposes, ceased to be, and
not being, they were wrong.

It was not necessary, however, for the political
thinkers of the eighteenth century to go back
directly to Aristotle and the Schoolmen. They
had what was for them a better authority nearer
home. Descartes, the most influential philosopher of his age, had reaffirmed the Aristotelian
and Scholastic doctrine in the most positive

7

terms. At the beginning of his *Discourse on Method* we read that ' what is called good sense or reason is equal in all men,' and a little later he says, ' I am disposed to believe that (reason) is to be found complete in each individual ; and on this point to adopt the opinion of philosophers who say that the difference of greater or less holds only among the accidents, and not among the forms or natures of individuals of the same species.' Descartes took not the slightest interest in politics, and was concerned only with physical science and the theory of knowledge. It remained for others to draw the obvious political conclusions from what was for him, as it had been for Aristotle and the Schoolmen, a purely abstract meta-physical principle. These conclusions might have been drawn at any time during the preceding two thousand years. But it was only during the two centuries immediately following Descartes' death that political circumstances in Europe, especially in France, were favourable to such conclusions being drawn. The forms of government current during classical antiquity and the Middle Ages had been efficient and well adapted to the circumstances of the times. They seemed, accordingly, right and reasonable. In the eight-eenth century, on the other hand, particularly on the continent of Europe, the existing form of government was not adapted to the social circumstances of the age. At a period when the middle classes were already rich and well educated, absolute monarchy and the ineffectual remains of feudalism were unsuitable as forms of government. Being unsuitable, they therefore seemed utterly unreasonable and wrong. Middle-class Frenchmen wanted a share in the government. But men are not content merely to desire ; they like to have a logical or pseudo-logical justification for their desires ; they like to believe that when they want something, it is not merely for their own personal advantage, but that their desires are dictated by pure reason, by nature, by God Himself. The greater part of the world's philosophy and theology is merely an intellectual justification for the wishes and the day-dreams of philosophers and theologians. And practically all political theories are elaborated, after the fact, to justify the interests and desires of certain individuals, classes, or nations. In the eighteenth century, middle-class Frenchmen justified their very natural wish to participate in the government of the country by elaborating a new political philosophy from the metaphysical doctrine of Aristotle, the Schoolmen, and Descartes. These philosophers had taught that the specific essence is the same in all individuals of a species. In the case of *Homo Sapiens* this specific essence is reason. All men are equally reasonable. It follows that all men have an equal capacity, and therefore an equal right, to govern ; there are no born slaves nor masters. Hence, monarchy and hereditary aristocracy are inadmissible.

Nature herself demands that government shall be organized on democratic principles. Thus middle-class Frenchmen had the satisfaction of discovering that their desires were endorsed as right and reasonable, not only by Aristotle, St. Thomas, and Descartes, but also by the Creator of the Universe in person.

MAKING THE FACTS FIT

Even metaphysicians cannot entirely ignore the obvious facts of the world in which they live. Having committed themselves to a belief in this fundamental equality of all men, the eighteenth-century political philosophers had to invent an explanation for the manifest inequalities which they could not fail to observe on every side. If Jones, they argued, is an imbecile and Smith a man of genius, that is due, not to any inherent and congenital differences between the two men, but to purely external and accidental differences in their upbringing, their education, and the ways in which circumstances have compelled them to use their minds. Give Jones the right sort of training, and you can turn him into a Newton, a St. Francis, or a Caesar according to taste. 'The diversity of opinions,' says Descartes, ' does not arise from some being endowed with a larger share of reason than others, but solely from this, that we conduct our thoughts along different ways, and do not fix our atten-

THE IDEA OF EQUALITY

tion on the same objects.' 'Intelligence, genius, and virtue,' says Helvétius, whose work, *De l'Esprit*, was published in 1758, and exercised an enormous contemporary influence, 'are the products of education.' And again (*De l'Esprit*, Discours III. ch. 26) : '*La grande inégalité d'esprit qu'on apperçoit entre les hommes dépend donc uniquement et de la différente éducation qu'ils reçoivent, et de l'enchaînement inconnu et divers dans lesquels ils se trouvent placés*,' and so on.

The political and philosophical literature of the eighteenth century teems with such notions. It was only to be expected ; for such notions, it is obvious, are the necessary corollaries of the Cartesian axiom that reason is the same and entire in all men. They followed no less necessarily from the *tabula rasa* theory of mind elaborated by Locke. Both philosophers regarded men as originally and in essence equal, the one in possessing the same specific faculties and innate ideas, the other in possessing no innate ideas. It followed from either assumption that men are made or marred exclusively by environment and education. Followers whether of Locke or of Descartes, the eighteenth-century philosophers were all agreed in attributing the observed inequalities of intelligence and virtue to inequalities of instruction. Men were naturally reasonable and therefore good ; but they lived in the midst of vice and abject superstition. Why ? because evil-minded legislators—kings

11

and priests—had created a social environment
calculated to warp the native reason and corrupt
the morals of the human race. Why priests and
kings, who, as human beings, were themselves
naturally reasonable and therefore virtuous,
should have conspired against their fellows, or
why their reasonable fellows should have allowed
themselves to be put upon by these crafty corrupters, was never adequately explained. The
democratic religion, like all other religions, is
founded on faith as much as on reason. The
king-priest theory in its wildest and most extrava-
gant form is the inspiration and subject of much
of Shelley's finest poetry. Poor Shelley, together
with large numbers of his less talented predecessors and contemporaries, seems seriously to
have believed that by getting rid of priests and
kings you could inaugurate the golden age.

THE TESTS OF EXPERIMENT

The historical and psychological researches of
the past century have rendered the theory which
lies behind the practice of modern democracy
entirely untenable Reason is not the same in
all men ; human beings belong to a variety of
psychological types separated one from another
by irreducible differences. Men are not the exclusive product of their environments. A century
of growing democracy has shown that the reform
of institutions and the spread of education are by

beggar man, thief,' he really means something like intelligent man, imbecile, mathematician and non-mathematician, musical person and unmusical person, etc. Presuming that this is what he does mean, let us examine the Behaviourists' hypothesis, which is identical with that of the philosophers who, in the eighteenth century, elaborated the theory of modern democracy. The first thing that strikes one about the Behaviourists' hypothesis is, that the observations on which it is based are almost exclusively observations on small children, not on fully grown men and women. It is on the ground that all infants are very much alike that the Behaviourists deny the hereditary transmission of special aptitudes, attributing the enormous differences of mental capacity observable among grown human beings exclusively to differences in environment, internal and external. Now it is an obvious and familiar fact, that the younger a child, the less individually differentiated it is. Physically, all new-born children are very much alike : there are few fathers who, after seeing their new-born infant once, could recognize it again among a group of other infants. Mr. Watson will not, I suppose, venture to deny that physical peculiarities may be inherited. Yet the son who at twenty will have his father's aquiline nose and his mother's dark, straight hair may be as snubnosed and golden at two as another child whose father is pugfaced and his mother blonde, and who will grow up to be like them. If the Behaviourists had made their observations on children a few months before they were born, they would have been able to affirm not only the psychological identity of all men and women, but also their physical identity. Three days after their respective conceptions, Pocohontas, Shakespeare, and a negro congenital idiot would probably be indistinguishable from one another, even under the most powerful microscope. According to Behaviourist notions, this should be regarded as a conclusive proof of the omnipotence of nurture. Since they are indistinguishable at conception, it must be environment that turns the fertilized ova into respectively a Red-Indian woman, an English man of genius, and a negro idiot.

Mind and body are closely interdependent : they come to maturity more or less simultaneously. A mind is not fully grown until the body with which it is connected through the brain has passed the age of puberty. The mind of a young child is as much undifferentiated and unindividualized as its body. It does not become completely itself until the body is more or less fully grown. A child of two has neither his father's nose nor his maternal grandfather's talent for mathematics. But that is no argument against his developing both when he is a few years older. A young child looks and thinks like other children of the same age and not like his parents. Later on he will certainly look like his parents. What reason is there to suppose that his mind will not also be like theirs? If he has his father's nose, why not also his father's brain, and with it his father's mentality. The Behaviourists give us no answer to those questions. They merely state, what we already knew, that small children are very much alike. But this is entirely beside the point. Two fertilized ova may be indistinguishable; but if one belongs to a negress and the other to a Japanese, no amount of nurture will make the Japanese egg develop into a negro or *vice versa*. There is no more valid reason for supposing that the two very similar infants who were to become Shakespeare and Stratford's village idiot could have been educated into exchanging their adult parts. To study human psychology exclusively in babies is like studying the anatomy of frogs exclusively in tadpoles. That environment may profoundly influence the course of mental development is obvious. But it is no less obvious that there is a hereditarily conditioned development to be modified. Environment no more creates a mental aptitude in a grown boy than it creates the shape of his nose.

EQUALITY OF VIRTUE

We have dealt so far with the primary assumption from which the whole theory and practice of democracy flows—that all men are substantially equal, and with one of its corollaries

—that the observed differences between human
beings are due to environment, and that education, in the widest sense of the term, is all
powerful. It is now necessary to touch briefly
on one or two other corollaries. Men being in
essence equally reasonable, it follows that they
are also in essence equally moral. For morality
(according to the philosophers who formulated
the theory of democracy) is absolute and exists
in itself, apart from any actual society of right-
or wrong-doing individuals. The truths of
morality can be apprehended by reason. All
men are equally reasonable : therefore all are
equally capable of grasping the absolute truths
of moral science. They are therefore, in essence,
equally virtuous, and if, in practice, they behave
badly, that is merely an accident, due to corrupting surroundings. Man must be delivered
from his corrupting surroundings (and for the
most ardent and the most ruthlessly logical
spirits all government, all law, and organized
religion are corrupting influences). Finding
himself once more in that idyllic ' state of nature '
from which he should never have tried to rise,
man will become, automatically, perfectly virtuous. There are few people now, I suppose, who
take the theories of Rousseau very seriously.
But though our intellect may reject them, our
emotions are still largely influenced by them.
Many people still cherish a vague sentimental
belief that the poor and uncultivated, who are

nearer to the 'state of nature' than the cultured and the rich, are for that reason more virtuous.

DEMOCRATIC POT AND CATHOLIC KETTLE

Pots have a diverting way of calling kettles black, and the prophets of the democratic-humanitarian religion have at all times, from the eighteenth century down to the present day, denounced the upholders of Christian orthodoxy as anti-scientific. In certain important respects, however, the dogmas and the practice of orthodox Catholic Christianity were and are more nearly in accordance with the facts than the dogmas and practice of democratic-humanitarianism. The doctrine of Original Sin is, scientifically, much truer than the doctrine of natural reasonableness and virtue. Original Sin, in the shape of anti-social tendencies inherited from our animal ancestors, is a familiar and observable fact. Primitively, and in a state of nature, human beings were not, as the eighteenth-century philosophers supposed, wise and virtuous : they were apes.

Practically, the wisdom of the Church displays itself in a recognition among human beings of different psychological types. It is not every Tom, Dick, or Harry who is allowed to study the intricacies of theology. What may strengthen the faith of one may bewilder or perhaps even disgust another. Moreover, not all are called upon to rule ; there must be discipline, a hierarchy, the subjection of many and the dominion of few. In these matters the theory and practice of the Church is based on observation and long experience. The humanitarian democrats who affirm that men are equal, and who on the strength of their belief distribute votes to everybody, can claim no experimental justification for their beliefs and actions. They are men who have a faith, and who act on it, without attempting to discover whether the faith corresponds with objective reality.

THE RELATION OF THEORY TO ACTION

It is in the theory of human equality that modern democracy finds its philosophical justification and some part, at any rate, of its motive force. It would not be true to say that the democratic movement took its rise in the theories propounded by Helvétius and his fellows. The origin of any widespread social disturbance is never merely a theory. It is only in pursuit of their interests, or under the influence of powerful emotions, that large masses of men are moved to action. When we analyse any of the historical movements in favour of democracy or self-determination, we find that they derive their original impetus from considerations of self-interest on the part of the whole or a part of the population. Autocracy

and the rule of foreigners are often (though by
no means invariably) inefficient, cruel, and corrupt. Large masses of the subjects of despots
or strangers find their interests adversely affected
by the activities of their rulers. They desire to
change the form of government, so that it shall
be more favourable to their particular national
or class interests. But the discontented are
never satisfied with mere discontent and desire
for change. They like, as I have already pointed
out, to justify their discontent, to find exalted
and philosophical excuses for their desires, to
feel that the state of affairs most convenient to
themselves is also the state of affairs most agreeable to Pure Reason, Nature, and the Deity.
Violent oppression begets violent and desperate
reaction. But if their grievances are only moderate, men will not fight whole-heartedly for their
redress, unless they can persuade themselves of
the absolute rightness, the essential reasonableness of what they desire. Nor will they be able,
without some kind of intellectual rationalization
of these desires, to persuade other men, with less
immediate cause for discontent, to join them.
Emotion cannot be communicated by a direct
contagion. It must be passed from man to man
by means of a verbal medium. Now words,
unless they are mere onomatopœic exclamations,
appeal to the emotions through the understanding. Feelings are communicated by means of
ideas, which are their intellectual equivalent ;

at the sound of the words conveying the ideas the appropriate emotion is evoked. Thus, theory is seen to be doubly important, first, as providing a higher, philosophical justification for feelings and wishes, and second, as making possible the communication of feeling from one man to another. 'The equality of all men' and 'natural rights' are examples of simple intellectual generalizations which have justified emotions of discontent and hatred, and at the same time have rendered them easily communicable. The rise and progress of any democratic movement may be schematically represented in some such way as this. Power is in the hands of a government that injures the material interests, or in some way outrages the feelings, of all, or at least an influential fraction of its subjects. The subjects are discontented and desire to change the existing government for one which shall be, for their purposes, better. But discontent and desire for change are not in themselves enough to drive men to action. They require a cause which they can believe to be absolutely, and not merely relatively and personally, good. By postulating (quite gratuitously) the congenital equality of all men, by assuming the existence of certain 'natural rights' (the term is entirely meaningless), existing absolutely, in themselves and apart from any society in which such rights might be exercised, the discontented are able to justify their discontent, and at the same time to communicate it by means of easily remembered intellectual formulas to their less discontented fellows.

THEORY GETS OUT OF HAND

The invention of transcendental reasons to justify actions dictated by self-interest, instinct, or prejudice would be harmless enough if the justificatory philosophy ceased to exist with the accomplishment of the particular action it was designed to justify. But once it has been called into existence, a metaphysic is difficult to kill. Men will not let it go, but persist in elaborating the system, in drawing with a perfect logic ever fresh conclusions from the original assumptions. These assumptions, which are accepted as axiomatic, may be demonstrably false. But the arguments by which conclusions are reached may be logically flawless. In that case, the conclusions will be what the logicians call ' hypothetically necessary.' That is to say that, granted the truth of the assumptions, the conclusions are necessarily true. If the assumptions are false the conclusions are necessarily false. It may be remarked in passing, that the hypothetical necessity of the conclusions of a logically correct argument has often and quite unjustifiably been regarded as implying the absolute necessity of the assumptions from which the argument starts.

In the case of the theory of democracy the

original assumptions are these : that reason is the same and entire in all men, and that all men are naturally equal. To these assumptions are attached several corollaries : that men are naturally good as well as naturally reasonable ; that they are the product of their environment ; and that they are indefinitely educable. The main conclusions derivable from these assumptions are the following : that the state ought to be organized on democratic lines ; that the governors should be chosen by universal suffrage ; that the opinion of the majority on all subjects is the best opinion ; that education should be universal, and the same for all citizens. The primary assumptions, as we have seen, are almost certainly false ; but the logic with which the metaphysicians of democracy deduced the conclusions was sound enough. Given the assumptions, the conclusions were necessary.

In the early stages of that great movement which has made the whole of the West democratic, there was only discontent and a desire for such relatively small changes in the mode of government as would increase its efficiency and make it serve the interests of the discontented. A philosophy was invented to justify the malcontents in their demands for change ; the philosophy was elaborated ; conclusions were relentlessly drawn ; and it was found that, granted the assumptions on which the philosophy was based, Logic demanded that the changes in the existing institutions should be, not small, but vast, sweeping, and comprehensive. Those who rationalize their desires for the purpose of persuading themselves and others that these desires are in accord with nature and reason find themselves persuading the world of the rightness and reasonableness of many ideas and plans of action of which they had, originally, never dreamed. Whatever is, is right. Becoming familiar, a dogma automatically becomes right. Notions which for one generation are dubious novelties become for the next absolute truths, which it is criminal to deny and a duty to uphold. The malcontents of the first generation invent a justifying philosophy. The philosophy is elaborated, conclusions are logically drawn. Their children are brought up with the whole philosophy (remote conclusion as well as primary assumption), which becomes, by familiarity, not a reasonable hypothesis, but actually a part of the mind, conditioning and, so to speak, canalizing all rational thought. For most people, nothing which is contrary to any system of ideas with which they have been brought up since childhood can possibly be reasonable. New ideas are reasonable if they can be fitted into an already familiar scheme, unreasonable if they cannot be made to fit. Our intellectual prejudices determine the channels along which our reason shall flow.

Of such systems of intellectual prejudices some seem merely reasonable, and some are sacred as well as reasonable. It depends on the kind of entity to which the prejudices refer. In general it may be said that intellectual prejudices about non-human entities appear to the holder of them as merely reasonable, while prejudices about human entities strike him as being sacred as well as reasonable. Thus, we all believe that the earth moves round the sun, and that the sun is at a distance of some ninety million miles from our planet. We believe, even though we may be quite incapable of demonstrating the truth of either of these propositions — and the vast majority of those who believe in the findings of modern astronomy do so as an act of blind faith, and would be completely at a loss if asked to show reasons for their belief. We have a prejudice in favour of modern astronomy. Having been brought up with it, we find it reasonable, and any new idea which contradicts the findings of contemporary astronomy strikes us as absurd. But it does not strike us as morally reprehensible. Our complex of what may be called astronomy-prejudices is only reasonable, not sacred.

THE NEARER, THE MORE SACRED

There was a time, however, when men's astronomy-prejudices were bound up with a great human activity—religion. For their contemporaries the ideas of Copernicus and Galileo

26

were not merely absurd, as contradicting the established intellectual prejudices, they were also immoral. The established prejudices were supported by high religious authority. For its devotees, the local and contemporary brand of religion is ' good,' ' sacred,' ' right,' as well as reasonable and true. Anything which contradicts any part of the cult is therefore not only false and unreasonable, but also bad, unholy, and wrong. As the Copernican ideas became more familiar, they seemed less frightful. Brought up in a heliocentric system, the religious folk of ensuing generations accepted without demur the propositions which to their fathers had seemed absurd and wicked. History repeated itself when, in the middle of the nineteenth century, Darwin published his *Origin of Species*. The uproar was enormous. The theory of natural selection seemed much more criminal than the Copernican theory of planetary motion. Wickedness in these matters is proportionate to the distance from ourselves. Copernicus and Galileo had propounded unorthodox views about the stars. It was a crime, but not a very grave one ; the stars are very remote. Darwin and the Darwinians propounded unorthodox views about man himself. Their crime was therefore enormous. The dislike of the Darwinian hypothesis is by no means confined to those who believe in the literal truth of the Book of Genesis. One does not have to be an orthodox Christian to object to what seems an assault on human dignity, uniqueness, and superiority.

DEMOCRACY AS A RELIGION

The prejudices in favour of democracy belong to the second class ; they seem, to those who cherish them, sacred as well as reasonable, morally right as well as true. Democracy is natural, good, just, progressive, and so forth. The opponents of it are reactionary, bad, unjust, anti-natural, etc. For vast numbers of people the idea of democracy has become a religious idea, which it is a duty to try to carry into practice in all circumstances, regardless of the practical requirements of each particular case. The metaphysic of democracy which was in origin the rationalization of certain French and English men's desires for the improvement of their governments, has become a universally and absolutely true theology which it is all humanity's highest duty to put into practice. Thus, India must have democracy, not because democratic government would be better than the existing undemocratic government — it would almost certainly be incomparably worse—but because democracy is everywhere and in all circumstances right. The transformation of the theory of democracy into theology has had another curious result : it has created a desire for progress in the direction of more democracy among numbers of people whose material interests are in no way harmed, and are even actively advanced, by the existing form of government which they desire to change. This spread of socialism among the middle classes, the spontaneous granting of humanitarian reforms by power-holders to whose material advantages it would have been to wield their power ruthlessly and give none of it away —these are phenomena which have become so familiar that we have almost ceased to comment on them. They show how great the influence of a theory can be when by familiarity it has become a part of the mind of those who believe in it. In the beginning is desire ; desire is rationalized ; logic works on the rationalization and draws conclusions ; the rationalization, with all these conclusions, undreamed of in many cases by those who first desired and rationalized, becomes one of the prejudices of the men of the succeeding generations ; the prejudice determines their judgment of what is right and wrong, true and false ; it gives direction to their thoughts and desires ; it drives them into action. The result is, that a man whose interests are bound up with the existing order of things will desire to make changes in that order much more sweeping than those desired by his grandfather, though the latter's material interests were genuinely injured by it. Man shall not live by bread alone. The divine injunction was unnecessary. Man never has lived by bread alone, but by every word that proceeded out of the mouth of every conceivable God. There are occasions when it would be greatly to man's advantage if he did confine himself for a little exclusively to bread.

VARIETIES OF INTELLIGENCE

WHAT IS INTELLIGENCE ?

Intelligence is one of these entities which the ordinary human being understands without being able to define. He is able in practice to distinguish an intelligent from an unintelligent person, a course of action which in any given circumstances bears witness to the possession of intelligence from one that does not. But any definition of intelligence which he could offer would almost certainly prove, on critical examination, to be erroneous or incomplete, and would quite certainly turn out to be useless from the point of view of the scientist. In the course of recent years professional psychologists have offered many definitions of intelligence. ' Conscious adaptation to new situations,' ' the capacity to learn,' ' the power to perceive the relations between ideas '—these are a few of the definitions suggested. All of them have been subjected to more or less destructive criticism. What precisely is intelligence ? Discussion still rages. The professionals seem to be unable to decide. Must the layman then refrain from using the still indefinite and perhaps meaningless word, from applying in practical life his conceptions regarding the nature of the thing ? I think not. The layman is justified in going on as he has always done ; he knows, for his own purposes, what he is talking about. The professionals have to a great extent created their own difficulties. If they find it hard to decide what intelligence is, that is solely because they are looking for some quality of the mind that can be isolated and quantitatively measured in the laboratory or class-room. Their failure to agree on a definition of intelligence does not prove that the layman is wrong in having his own vague but useful conceptions regarding its nature. What it proves, if it proves anything, is that intelligence is extremely difficult to isolate, and still more difficult to measure quantitatively.

I shall not attempt to offer a definition of intelligence. Life is so constituted that we can make effective use of things whose nature we do not understand. The lower animals comprehend nothing, and yet they contrive to live very successfully. It is the same with us. Even of the things we have most systematically investigated we know incredibly little. And yet we live ; and not only live, but invent sciences. We need not know a thing in order to be able to investigate and control it. Where knowledge is absent—and in an absolute sense we can know nothing—a vague working hypothesis is quite enough for all practical and even philosophical purposes. The popular conception of intelligence represents such a working hypothesis. By means of it we are able to explain, or at least co-ordinate, many of the observed facts of human existence. Where the practical affairs of life are concerned it is indispensably useful. In course of time, as our knowledge of the workings of the mind grows greater, the popular conception of intelligence will doubtless tend to become more accurate and precise, and its value as a working hypothesis will increase. Meanwhile, however, our own conception must necessarily suffice us. We all know intuitively what intelligence is, and we act on that knowledge, more or less successfully. I use the word here in its contemporary popular sense, the sense in which we all use it and in accordance with which we judge the actions and characters of men. The word connotes too much to admit of simple definition ; but when we see it, we all know what it means.

INTELLIGENCE IN RELATION TO THE
WHOLE PERSONALITY

In making practical judgments we never completely isolate the intelligence from the rest of the personality. Practical judgments deal with life, and, in life, the organism functions as a whole. A constituent part is seldom if ever found acting in complete isolation from the rest. It is only in an abstract analysis and not in life that the intelligence can be separated from the other elements, psychological and physiological, of the

33

whole personality. The way in which intelligence is applied is determined to a very great extent by the state of the body, by the instincts, the emotions, and those composite sentiments organized in every individual by the influence of tradition and education acting on the native psychological material. The way in which intelligence is applied depends, in a word, on health and character. We are all familiar with the clever people who make no use of their talents, owing to some feebleness of impulse, some impotence of emotion, some defect in the will or fault in its training. In many cases a physiological defect accompanies and perhaps determines these spiritual weaknesses, which are often remedied when health is improved. Much, too, depends on the physical temperament of the individual. Temperament (and with it the way intelligence is used) may be altered by changes in the environment involving changes in the hitherto normal functioning of the ductless glands. During the war, for example, many men who had up till then led sheltered and sedentary lives ' discovered,' to use Cannon's phrase, ' their adrenals,' and discovering their adrenals changed their temperament and the modality of their intelligence. It is, I repeat, only in the abstract that we can discuss the varieties of intelligence without considering the varieties in the other constituents of the physico-psychological personality. In practice there is all the difference in the world between two intrinsically similar intelligences, one of which happens to be connected with a mental and bodily organism that is healthy, active, and well-trained, the other with an ill-trained, sickly, and inactive organism. When the time comes to make practical applications, these differences in effectiveness between similar intelligences will, of course, be taken into account. In the present essay I shall deal abstractly with the intelligence considered in itself and apart from what it achieves or fails to achieve in actual life.

ON ABSTRACTIONS

An abstraction can never be true. To abstract is to select certain aspects of reality regarded as being, for one reason or another, significant. The aspects of reality not selected do not thereby cease to exist, and the abstraction is therefore never a true, in the sense of a complete, picture of reality. It is the very incompleteness of the picture that makes it valuable for us. Reality is so immeasurably complicated that it is impossible for us to comprehend it synthetically in entirety. Abstraction provides us with a series of humanly significant and comprehensible simplifications. If we have understood these abstract sketches of certain aspects of an object, we can return to the reality with a better chance of understanding it as a whole. It is necessary, however, to avoid the mistakes so frequently made by men of science in the past — the mistake of treating the abstractions of scientific analysis as though they were true pictures, and of regarding as non-existent those aspects of reality which the maker of the abstractions has chosen to omit. The present essay is an abstract sketch, extremely rough, as I am only too well aware, and very inadequate, of human intelligence in certain of its varieties. It contains many bold statements and sweeping generalizations—statements and generalizations which I do not regard as being true without qualification (if all the necessary qualifications were made, all the fine distinctions drawn, this book would swell to a monstrous size), but true enough in the main to provide a working hypothesis for the practical judgment of individuals and social institutions.

THE CLASSICAL VIEW

It was from Aristotle's doctrine of the substantial identity of all members of a species that Descartes and the eighteenth-century philosophers deduced the identity in all men of reason or good sense. They were confirmed in this belief by the fact that there is only one logic. Seeing that there is only one way of getting from a major premiss to a conclusion, they imagined that the intelligences which followed this identical road must themselves be identical. A fallacy. For though there is only one road from a premiss to a conclusion, there are many premisses. Intelligences differ one from another, not in the way they reason, but in the kind of major premisses they choose to reason from. One mind will find it entirely natural to choose one kind of major premiss : to another this kind of premiss will seem intrinsically absurd. Newman has summarized the whole matter with his usual force and subtlety. ' All reasoning being from premisses, and these premisses arising (if it so happens) in their first elements from personal characteristics, in which men are in fact in essential and irremediable variance one with another, the ratiocinative talent can do no more than point out where the difference between them lies, how far it is immaterial, when it is worth while continuing an argument between them, and when not.' It is an important and significant fact that there should be only one way of reaching a conclusion from a given major premiss. But it is no less important and significant that there should be no single criterion for judging major premisses, but that every man should select his own on personal and ultimately irrational grounds. In the present essay I shall describe a few of the principal varieties of intelligence ; I shall give examples of the kind of major premisses naturally selected by individuals of each type, and shall try to show in what way the prevailing fashions in major premisses may affect their choice.

HORIZONTAL AND VERTICAL CLASSIFICATION
OF MINDS

Intelligences can be arranged according to two systems of classification—a horizontal system and a vertical one. In other words, intelligences differ to some extent in kind, as well as in amount and degree of excellence. Two minds may occupy the same position in the ordinarily accepted scale of values, but may be widely different in kind. Two others may be of the same kind, but may occupy positions at opposite ends of the scale of values. Thus, the intelligence, say, of William James may be regarded as standing at about the same height in the scale of values as the intelligence, say, of Hegel, but at a considerable distance horizontally from it. The mind of Sinclair Lewis's creation, Babbitt, occupies a position vastly below that of William James's mind ; but it belongs to the same kind. The vertical distance between them is great, but there is little horizontal difference. Similarly the vertical difference between Hegel and Joanna Southcott is enormous ; but the horizontal distance is very small.

Some horizontal as well as some vertical differences between intelligences are innate. Others are acquired. The innate differences may, to some extent, be modified by education. Conversely, external influences are differently received by congenitally different minds. In the present essay I shall try to distinguish between a few of the more important types of intelligence. Beginning with the characteristics that are innate, I shall discuss, first the horizontal differences between mind and mind, and then the vertical. The latter part of the essay will be devoted to a study of the way in which education, in the widest sense of the word, may create horizontal differences between intelligences.

THE EQUALITARIANS AND OURSELVES

During what may be called the democratic period of European history, philosophers went to endless trouble in order to prove that men were equal, and that the faculties were uniformly distributed throughout the human species. Their arguments were rationalizations either of their wish to improve the existing form of government by participating in it, or else (in the later part of the epoch) of their desire to justify what had already been done in the way of democratizing social institutions. In exactly the same way the contemporary arguments against human equality are largely rationalizations after the fact of our disappointment with the results of political democracy and of our desire, either to change the form of government, or to justify such changes as have already been made. An argument is none the worse for being the rationalization of a desire. Indeed, if we had no desires to rationalize, few arguments would ever be constructed. The truth or falsity (as distinct from the usefulness) of the rationalization must be judged without reference to the desire, feeling, or impulse to which it gives intellectual expression, or the action, the state of affairs which it justifies. Judged on its own merits, by the criterion of correspondence with the objective facts, the rationalization of our desires is superior to the rationalization of the desires of our eighteenth-century ancestors. Which is not, of course, to deny that our ancestors did a great and, to a considerable extent, a beneficial work in rationalizing as they did.

It was only, then, during the democratic period of European history that the doctrine of the equality of men and the uniform distribution of the faculties among all individuals of the human species was ever seriously maintained. Our reaction to this doctrine is in the nature of a return to the views prevailing before the democratic epoch—to the views on which even during that epoch every sane human being (including the philosophers who preached equality) must always have acted. The *consensus gentium* in favour of any proposition is not a proof of its objective truth. But it can never be entirely neglected : it has always some significance. For what it is worth, then, the *consensus gentium* throughout history is on our side, and opposed to the eighteenth-century equalitarians. What our generation has done is to systematize the vague conceptions of earlier times and to measure, so far as measurement is at present feasible, the differences between the various psychological types. A mere feeling or intuition cannot be directly communicated. It must be given an intellectual form before it can be expressed and understood. The practical intuition of inequality in the distribution of faculties was rationalized (whenever it *was* rationalized and not just dumbly acted upon) in terms of the medical theory of humours and the political theory of feudalism. Both are crude and inadequate. We have given to the intuition of inequality a somewhat more realistic intellectual expression, and have thereby rendered it more easily communicable and therefore more potentially effective.

THE CLASSIFICATION OF JUNG

The most interesting, and certainly the most complete, work yet written about the varieties of the human mind is Jung's *Psychological Types*. Jung's merit is not that he is a systematist; indeed, he systematizes a little too much. Psychology is too young a science to be systematic; and its subject-matter is too multifarious and

complicated to admit—as yet, at any rate—
of very exact classification. Jung inspires confidence because he is a psychologist born as
well as made. Reading his books, you feel that
here is a man who does genuinely understand
human beings in the profound intuitive way in
which a good novelist, like Tolstoi or Dostoievsky,
understands them. I know of no other professional psychologist of whom one feels the same.
Others know their business well enough ; but
Jung seems really to understand, not merely with
the intellect, but with his whole being, intimately
and intuitively. And he is not only an intuitive
knower of human nature ; he is also an acute
analyst, a philosopher, and a scholar. The psychologist who would tell us something significant
must be possessed of a multiplicity of talents.

Jung has divided human beings into two main
types, the introvert and the extravert. The
extravert's mental activity is directed outwards
towards the object, which dominates all his
thinking and feeling. The introvert retires from
the outer world, which he feels to be alien and
even hostile. Looking inwards, he finds in his
own thoughts, feelings, and imaginations about
the object a higher degree of reality than in
the object itself, as perceived by his senses. In
other words, reality for him is his reaction to his
sense-perceptions, not the perceptions themselves.
When the introvert considers external objects,
he demands that they shall fit into the emotional

or intellectual scheme which he has elaborated in his mind. The extravert, on the other hand, demands that the inward life shall adapt itself to the observed facts of the objective world. Each is a Procrustes ; but the victim of one is the other's torturing bed, his bed the other's victim. For the introvert, external objects are mere ephemeral irrelevances, not to be compared in significance and durability with the creations of the spirit. For the extravert, a thought or an imagination not canalized, so to speak, in an objective channel is a mere fantasy. The members of either type regard one another with incomprehension and mistrust. Hence the bitterness and inconclusiveness of the disputes between rival schools of philosophy. Platonists and Aristotelians, Realists and Nominalists, Idealists and Pragmatists—they have been fighting for centuries. The battle is in all cases between introverts and extraverts. The contrasted systems of philosophy are the expressions of differently orientated psychologies, of incompatible intellectual temperaments. In elaborating their respective dogmas—and one can be made as logically water-tight and unanswerable as the other—the rival philosophers use the same process of reasoning. They differ in their spontaneous choice of major premisses. One regards it as natural to suppose that the outside world is more real and significant than the inside ; the other finds it equally natural to suppose that the inside world is more real than the outside. Both, no doubt, are right, and both, in their exclusiveness of belief, are wrong.

Philosophy is only one of the battle-fields on which the opponents wage their secular warfare. With the same bitterness, the same lack of mutual comprehension as they display when arguing about metaphysics, introverts and extraverts do battle over religion, over recreations, over the social intercourse of daily life. How far the types can be reconciled, how far either extraversion or introversion as a mental attitude, a habit of thought, can be imposed on minds of an opposite tendency, are questions which will be discussed later in this essay. At present it is enough to have recorded the existence of the two inborn and contrasting dispositions.

EXTREME CASES

The peculiarities of the introvert intelligence are most clearly shown when it attempts to deal, in terms of its inner life, with objects outside itself. Similarly, the extraverted mind reveals itself most unmistakably when it strays on to the proper domain of the introvert. As an example of the introvert dealing with objective facts in an introverted way, we may select Hegel. In his *Nature Philosophy* Hegel professes to be dealing with objective facts. But he proceeds from

within outwards, trying to impose his own inward
conception of what the universe ought to be
on the external phenomena. The oracular pro-
nouncement contained in his thesis, *De Orbitis
Planetarum*, is justly celebrated. Speaking from
the clouds of his own private and Platonic Sinai,
he announced that it was impossible, in the
nature of things, that there should be a planet
between Mars and Jupiter. Almost simultaneously the astronomer Piazzi discovered the
asteroid Ceres. His other scientific achievements are hardly less remarkable. In the following passage Hegel is speaking of light and the
transparency or opacity of material substances.
' Light,' he says, ' is abstract identity and completely free. Air is the identity of the elements.
Subordinate identity is an identity passive to
light ; hence the transparency of the diamond.
Metal, on the contrary, is opaque, because in it
individual identity is concentrated in a profounder
unity by a high specific weight.' That the specific
weight of the diamond is higher than that of
several metals is a matter of relatively small
importance. What is significant about the
passage I have quoted is the prevailing tone, the
fundamental assumption underlying it. Hegel
assumes that the outside world must be modelled
on the dialectic universe within his mind, ' What
I think three times is objectively true.' That is
what, in effect, he is affirming. That our conception of the universe is necessarily a human

conception is obvious ; we cannot look at the world through the eyes of ants or of omniscient spirits. The universe that we know is to some extent created by ourselves. But this is not to affirm that the outside world is dependent on us ; that it obeys our dialectic and dances to abracadabrical formulae about abstract and subordinate identity. It will be sufficiently clear from the foregoing remarks that, being myself, in intellectual matters, a moderate extravert, and having been brought up to believe in an extraverted philosophy of the world, I am congenitally and by training incapable of understanding what Hegel means. *The Nature Philosophy* reads for me like the ravings of a lunatic. And yet there were, and I believe still are, Hegelians for whom the book is full of the profoundest significance.

Being myself, as I have said, a moderate extravert, I am able to understand the activities of the extravert when he ventures on to the introvert's domain much better than I can understand the introvert's activities among external facts. Thus the extravert who ' explains ' religion in terms of the observable facts of physiology and instinctive psychology is doing something which, for me, is perfectly comprehensible and natural. To impose the standards of the outward objective world upon the inner world strikes me as an obviously sensible process. Some souls are *naturaliter Christianae* : others are congenitally

46

materialistic. Mine belongs to the latter category. I understand the materialist interpretation of inward life. But the introvert Procrustes, who would chop and trim the objective world in order that it may fit the bed he has prepared for it in his mind, seems to me a monster. To understand sympathetically, with one's whole being, the state of mind of some one radically unlike oneself is very difficult—is, so far as I am concerned, impossible. No less difficult is it to deny, whole-heartedly, the validity of mental processes naturally similar to one's own. The intellect, however, is able to make the necessary corrections, not in the realm of living intuition, but, at any rate, in that of theory. That the typical extravert interpretation of subjective happenings is beset with serious philosophic objections is something which even an extraverted intellect can understand. Thus, I am unable to agree intellectually with all the conclusions of an extraverted and materialist interpreter of religion, like Mr. James Leuba, for example, though I find myself naturally sympathetic with his outlook on the world.

PERSONAL TOUCHES

In discussing psychological matters it is difficult to avoid the personal touch. Knowing for certain only one's own reactions to the outside world, only one's own modes of thought and

47

feeling, one is almost compelled to talk about oneself. And perhaps, after all, psychologists ought to talk about themselves. For it is more modest and truthful to admit what is in fact the case—that one can speak only for oneself, and perhaps for those congenitally like oneself —than to pretend to a position of superior neutrality which one does not and cannot occupy. In the war between the types there can be no Monsieur Romain Rolland *au-dessus de la mêlée*. There are no psychological Scandinavians or Swiss. You cannot conscientiously object to taking sides in the quarrel : you are a combatant whether you like it or not, because nature has conscribed you on one side or another —there are many sides in the confused battle of the minds — before even you were born. The only honest thing to do is to admit your spiritual nationality, and either fight for your cause or else, if you don't want to fight, admit the irreconcilable differences between yourself and your opponents, and agree to differ without any more superfluous argumentation. This must be my justification for mentioning my own re-actions to doctrines and modes of expression invented by other minds. It is by pointing out what seems strange or incomprehensible to me that I can most satisfactorily illustrate my generalization about the diversity of types.

THE ABSOLUTE

If I had to define my position in relation to Jung's system of the co-ordinates, I should say that I was a moderately extraverted intellectual. My natural tendency is to cut the cloth of my inner life to fit the objective world of things and current ideas. I have no dislike or fear of external objects, and feel no objection to immersing myself in them. For this reason I find incomprehensible the state of mind of those to whom the flux of reality seems something dreadful and repulsive. Enjoying my bath in the flux, I feel no longing for rocks of ages or other similar eternal solidities. I am in my element in the current, and pant for no dry land. There are many people who feel all the hymn-writer's distress at seeing ' change and decay in all around.' I am not one of them. Nor would it naturally occur to me to seek a comfort, of which I do not feel the need, from the contemplation of something changeless. Intellectually I am able to understand the doctrine, for example, of Platonic ideas ; but I am unable to discover in myself any intimate reason for believing it. That the Absolute exists is not one of the major premisses I should spontaneously have thought of. For the Absolute, psychologically speaking, is the introvert's subjective compensation for the multifariousness of strange and hostile objects. Those to whom objects seem friendly, and who enjoy the kaleidoscopic panorama of the outside world, feel no need of an Absolute. The introvert dislikes objects and regards them as inferior to his thoughts in importance and reality. The major premiss which an extravert would spontaneously choose to reason from is very different. For him things genuinely exist, and are more real than his thoughts about them.

The doctrine of the Absolute is an intellectual doctrine, and one, consequently, which I can understand with the reasoning part of me, even if I cannot realize in myself the state of mind of which it is a rationalization. But introverts are not always intellectuals, and when they are not, I find the greatest difficulty in understanding them. One of the most lucid sentences in M. André Breton's *Poisson Soluble* is the following. '*Quand je lui dis : " Prends ce verre fumé qui est ma main dans tes mains, voici l'éclipse," elle sourit et plonge dans les mers pour en ramener la branche de corail du sang*' A little thought enables me to reconstruct the scene of which this is a description : a hand is put in front of the woman's eyes ; against the sunlight she sees the fingers bright red, as though they were branches of coral. Understanding M. Breton's method in this sentence, I can see why I do not understand him in most of the rest of his work. What he writes about is never the object as directly perceived, but the fancies which the object evokes in his mind. At times (as in the sentence quoted above) the fancies are of a kind which might occur to me. (But if they did occur to me, I should never write directly and exclusively of the fancies, as though they were the only things that mattered ; I should write of the objects themselves and should only bring in the fancies as illustrative or decorative similes.) Most of the time, however, M. Breton's fancies are of such a kind that my prosaic mind is unable to perceive the connection between his words and the objects of which he is indirectly talking. Few introverted writers, it is true, have the courage of their introversion to the same extent as M. Breton. A *Surréaliste*, he is on principle entirely careless of the outside world and of his readers. Most introverts make certain concessions to the objective world when they appear in public. It is generally in private intercourse, when they are being quite frankly themselves, that the extravert is made aware of their spiritual remoteness. Few things are more disquieting than to discover, on the evidence of some casual remark, that you are talking to a person whose mind is radically alien to your own. Between one easy chair in front of the fire and another a gulf suddenly yawns ; you must have a strong head to be able to look into it without feeling giddy.

EXTRAVERTED TYPES

Certain types of extreme extravert are no less incomprehensible to me than the introverts. The

really sociable man, who is only happily himself
when he is in company, is to me a very mysterious figure. That people should be able to live
without privacy and solitude strikes me as extraordinary. And how repulsive, how incomprehensible I find the philosophy which is the
rationalization of these people's outward-looking
passion for their fellows ! It is a philosophy
which exalts the crowd at the expense of the
individual, which makes happiness synonymous
with the social pleasures, which explains individual morality exclusively in terms of social
need, which makes of religion a primarily communal activity. The major premisses of this
philosophy are of a kind which it would never
occur to me to choose, and though I understand it intellectually, I lack all living and
sympathetic comprehension of its meaning.
There is no disputing about tastes ; and equally,
there is no disputing, after a certain point
has been reached, about reasons. The only
theories about which it is possible to argue
with any hope of reaching a definite conclusion are those which can be directly tested by
experiment.

Another type of pronounced extravert, whose
outlook on life I find it impossible to understand
except theoretically, is the type of man who
lives for sensations rather than for ideas or
emotions. For these people, the pure sensation
is so delightful, and seems in its intensity so

significant, that the cultivation of sensations is a completely satisfying end in itself. The merely animal sensualist is a gross, dull fellow, not worth talking about. The interesting specimen of this type is the refined and conscious aesthete, who is intelligent enough to have the desire and the power to rationalize his love of sensations into a philosophy. Morality for this exquisite sensationalist is a branch of aesthetics. Actions are good because they are elegant. Religion he admires only for its trappings — because the religious rite is a kind of ballet or spectacular charade. Art is robbed of its philosophical and moral significance and reduced to a matter of pure aesthetics ; he exalts it nevertheless as the most important of human activities. Ideas themselves, if they are cultivated, are treated as though they were a kind of sensations. Philosophy becomes frankly an art. Doctrines are collected for the sake of their charm, as though they were bronzes or carved jades : he arranges them in systems as a connoisseur might arrange pieces of china in a cabinet. Oscar Wilde's is a typical extravert-sensationalist's philosophy. I understand what he writes, but can discover no personal reason in myself for accepting his major premisses. Indeed, when I read a book by Wilde, I feel the most intimate personal reasons for rejecting them.

PROPER STUDIES

PRACTICALITY

Men and women differ in the extent to which they are practical. Some (and they seem to be the majority) are primarily interested in action ; others in contemplation. Some have a liking and a knack for doing things ; others shrink from practical tasks, and when they are compelled to perform them, perform them badly. One would be inclined to think, *a priori*, that practicality ought to be associated with extraversion and a contemplative tendency with introversion ; but I doubt whether such a correlation invariably holds. My own thinking is predominantly extraverted ; but I have a great dislike of practical activity. I am interested in the outside world, but only intellectually, not practically. My ambition and my pleasure are to understand, not to act ; and when action becomes necessary, I grudge the time I must devote to doing things in a world which I desire only intellectually to comprehend. Here, then, is at least one case of non-practical extraversion. I could cite the complementary case of a writer of my acquaintance. An introvert if ever there was one, he imposes his thinking and feeling on the outside world in a manner which, in our predominantly extraverted age, seems very eccentric. This habit of extreme introversion does not, however, prevent my friend from delighting in the practical life of the garden, the

54

workshop, and the farm. In the Utopias of William Morris or of Tolstoi he would be happy. To me the craftsman-ideal is simply a nightmare. I should go mad or commit suicide if I were compelled to waste my time (for in my eyes it would be a waste) making my own boots and buttons, growing my own vegetables, building my own house. There is no doubt that we have here a genuine plane of cleavage through the mass of humanity. Men and women can be divided up into two classes, consisting of those (the more numerous) with a bias towards practicality and those with a bias away from it. This plane of cleavage does not necessarily correspond with the extravert-introvert plane. In classifying any given individual we should have to fix his place in both categories.

VISUALIZERS AND OTHERS

Galton in his book on Human Faculties drew a distinction between two types of mind, which, though less profoundly significant than that between introvert and extravert, is yet of some importance. He showed that human beings can be classed as visualizers and non-visualizers. The visualizers think in terms of images seen with the mind's eye. The non-visualizers think abstractly, in terms of words which do not evoke definite images. It is extremely difficult for a person having one type of mind to under-

stand the workings of a mind of the opposite
type. I am myself a very imperfect visualizer.
By making an effort of will, I am able to conjure
up before my mind's eye images of a moderate
clarity and vividness. But images do not come
to me spontaneously. I think normally in terms
of words which represent an analysis of the
thing I am thinking of. Sometimes, even, it
seems to me that I think directly in terms of that
analysis without employing words at all. But
of this I cannot be certain. In any case, when
I wish to form a mental image, I do so piece-
meal, by putting together the analysis of the
thing I want to see, and translating it deliberately into visual terms. When I have to calcu-
late, I do so abstractly, without seeing the
digits or representing them to myself as having
any particular position in space. How different
is this from the procedure of the born visualizer !
I have supplemented Galton's description of the
type by personal inquiries among my acquaintance, with the result that I know (in theory)
fairly exactly how the visualizer thinks. My
only practical experiences of visualizing have
been during attacks of influenza. When my
temperature is in the neighbourhood of a hundred
and three, I begin to see mental images with
hallucinating clarity. The slightest external
stimulus brings them upon me in troops ; and
once established in my mind, these importunate
images proceed forthwith to lead in it a life of

their own, over which I have no voluntary control. When my blood cools, my thinking returns to its normal abstractness. On the strength of these experiences, I feel profoundly thankful that I am not congenitally a visualizer. It is unfair, of course, to judge the experiences of health by the standards of sickness : visualizing when the temperature is normal is not the same as visualizing under the influence of fever. It is not the same ; but to judge from what people in whom the tendency to visualize is strongly marked have told me, it must be different only in degree, not in kind. The pronounced visualizer lives perpetually in the company of his images, he cannot escape from them. Every word that he hears or reads, evokes in him a picture which has a life and duration of its own and is, to some extent, independent of the visualizer's control. I know one visualizer who finds it extraordinarily difficult to learn a piece of poetry by heart, because the images evoked by the poetry are so vivid that she cannot, even by making an effort of the will, get beyond them to the words by which they were called into existence. Thus, the words ' magic casements, opening on the foam of perilous seas, in faery lands forlorn,' will produce in her mind an overwhelmingly real and vivid image of windows in a strange house built into a cliff above the breakers. The image will be faithfully remembered, but not the words, which possess for the

57

visualizer only the value of picture-evokers. When it comes to translating the images back into words, the phrase 'mysterious windows looking on to the waves' will present itself just as readily as 'magic casements opening on the foam' — more readily, indeed, since Keats's words are the words of a poet, hence unique, original, and unlike the words that would naturally occur to some one who was not Keats. A pronounced visualizer is to a considerable extent at the mercy of his visualizations. When he has to think of something which lends itself to a mental treatment in terms of images, he is at an advantage over the non-visualizer, or at any rate on an equality with him : for it may be remarked that, for the purposes of effective thinking, abstract analysis in terms of words is almost always adequate. When the visualizer has to deal with subjects which do not lend themselves to treatment in terms of images, he finds himself at a loss. The images which his fancy arbitrarily creates at the sound or sight of words exclusively occupy his mind ; they stand between him and the matter about which he has to think. He sees, not the abstract idea, but only the often quite irrelevant pictures which the exposition of the idea has evoked in him. The strength and the weakness of the visualizer's position is clearly shown in his relation to numbers. All pronounced visualizers see numbers arranged in a definite and, for each individual, an unvary-

ing position in space. This number-form is
frequently coloured. The visualizer calculates
by looking at the form and with his mind's eye
reading off the figures. Visualizers whose
number-form is very definite, and includes a
great range of even very large numbers, can
perform mental calculations with great rapidity
and efficiency. It is probable that most calculating prodigies work on a visualized number-form.
In many cases, however, the number-form
is clearly seen only through the lower range of
numbers. Thus I have known visualizers who
could see all the figures from one to a thousand
quite clearly. After a thousand, however, the
numbers became dim and blurred. The result
was, that they found the task of calculating in
large sums extremely arduous. Being unable to
' see ' the large numbers, they found it almost
impossible to realize them. Comprehension was
confined within the limits of the visible form.
What was invisible they could not intuitively
understand. To them a hundred thousand and
a million, being both outside the form, seemed
for all practical purposes the same.

GEOMETERS AND ANALYSTS

Analogous to the difference between visualizer
and non-visualizer is that which in the realm
of mathematics separates the geometrical from
the analytical mind. Henri Poincaré was the

first, I believe, to point out the fundamental dissimilarity of these two types of mathematical intelligence. Some mathematicians are by nature geometrically minded ; they do their thinking predominantly in terms of figures and diagrams. Lord Kelvin confessed that he was incapable of understanding any physical hypothesis which he could not interpret schematically by means of a mechanical model. Clerk Maxwell's electromagnetic theory of light, which no human ingenuity could illustrate by mechanical models, remained for Kelvin incomprehensible to the last. There are other mathematicians, on the contrary, who think most easily in terms of pure abstraction, and to whom a model or a concrete diagram of any kind seems an obstacle to comprehension rather than an aid. Proofs which strike a Maxwell or an Henri Poincaré as overwhelmingly convincing leave a Kelvin sceptical. The reason of the born geometer is not the same as the reason of the born analyst.

It would add greatly to the symmetry of our classification if all visualizers were extraverts and all non-visualizers introverts, or *vice versa*. But though the temptation to make a neat job is strong, I can see no justification in the observable facts for succumbing to it. The tendencies to extraversion and introversion, visualizing and its opposite, are not invariably associated. The divisions which separate the types run along different lines. Some visualizers are introverts,

some are extraverts. There seems to be no
general rule.

THE TALENTED AND THE UNTALENTED

It is not hard to discover yet other planes of
cleavage in the mass of humanity. There are,
for example, special talents, the possession of
which separates a man in the most definite
manner from his untalented fellows. The
musical faculty is one of these talents, the
mathematical another. The complete absence
of either of these talents is rare. I have known,
however, at least two people of much more than
ordinary intelligence who were quite literally
unable to distinguish *Pop goes the weasel* from
God Save the King, except by the fact that the
weasel was not stood up for ; and several others,
by no means stupid, who could not pass the
simplest examination in elementary geometry
and algebra.

Such absolutely unmusical and unmathe-
matical people are the exceptions. The majority
of men and women are at least moderately gifted
in both these directions. But their gifts, when
compared with those of a Mozart or a Gauss,
are so negligible that their musical and mathematical intelligence may be regarded as different,
not merely in degree, but even in kind, from
that of the men of genius. I am myself tolerably musical—that is to say, I enjoy music

and, I think, comprehend it. But I am as utterly in the dark about the workings of a mind like Beethoven's as a dog is in the dark about the workings of my mind. No mental experience of my own avails me to form the slightest idea of what it must be like to have a mind that cogitates in terms of such things as the fugal opening of the C-sharp minor quartet and the slow movement of the Ninth Symphony. In the same way, I am quite unable even to imagine how Professor Einstein thinks. One must have some basis of experience on which to build an imagination, and I have no such basis. As a dog is to me, so am I musically to Beethoven and mathematically to Einstein. The only consolation is that Beethoven himself is a mathematical dog in relation to Einstein, while in all cases where visual art is concerned, Einstein on his own confession is a dog in comparison with any good painter or even any appreciator of painting.

VERTICAL DIFFERENCES

Other horizontal differences between intelligences might certainly be mentioned. But this essay does not profess to be comprehensive and systematic. My aim has been simply to show that horizontal differences in kind do really exist. The instances I have given are sufficient to substantiate the claim. The time has now come to say something about the vertical differences between intelligences. The vertical differences between intelligences have always and everywhere been recognized. That some men are born half-wits and some have one-and-a-half wits, that some are endowed with normal (in the sense of the numerically most common) capacities and some with capacities abnormally great or small — these are propositions which every sane man, when making practical judgments, has at all times assumed to be true. It is only by those who, like the Behaviourists or the eighteenth-century equalitarians, have had some theoretical or political axe to grind, that their truth has ever been doubted—and then, we can be perfectly sure, only in the abstract, never in practice. To prove the obvious is a waste of time. I shall assume, like every one else, that the vertical differences between human intelligences really exist, and proceed at once to a discussion of the various attempts made to measure these differences.

The Chinese were the first people, so far as is known, to attempt systematically to measure intelligence. Students were subjected to examinations from as early as the twelfth century before our era, and the successful candidates were given posts in the Civil Service. These examinations, like all that have been devised since, were tests of knowledge as well as of intelligence, of the capacity to profit by a scholastic training as well as of pure mother wit. But, as the world is arranged, knowledge and the power to acquire and remember it happen to be valuable, while the capacity to profit by scholastic training is much the same as the capacity which enables the man of average ability to lead an efficient and socially useful life. Many distinguished artists and great men of action have been very poor examinees ; but this does not militate against the scholastic examination as a test of the kind of intelligence found useful in ordinary social circumstances. The Chinese in their examination system laid great stress on original composition in verse and prose. According to modern educational psychologists, they were well inspired ; for the capacity to compose well is now regarded as the most important single sign of intelligence.

INTELLIGENCE TESTS

Of recent years, much ingenuity has been expended in devising intelligence tests that shall isolate mother wit from attainments and measure it as it is in itself without relation to the training it has received. That the attempt has not succeeded is clearly shown by the fact that children who have received a partial and irregular education, such as those of the gipsies and the canal-boat workers, are invariably, according to the intelligence tests, of lower mental age than regularly educated children of a corresponding chronological age. It may be doubted whether the perfect test of pure and isolated intelligence will ever be invented. The mind—hereditary make-up and acquired attainments—is an organic whole. It is as difficult, in practice, to isolate for examination a single part of the mental whole as it is to do the same for a single part of the physical organism. Indeed, it is more difficult in the case of the mind. For the part that the intelligence-testers would isolate is not an organ with a specific shape and position, like the liver or the spleen, but rather the sum of the activities of the whole mind working in one particular way and for the achievement of one particular set of results—intelligent action or rational thought. The idea that pure intelligence, apart from attainments and character, can be tested, so to speak, in the void is probably chimerical.

There are other objections to the existing tests. People whose minds work slowly — and many slow workers are far from stupid— cannot be expected to reveal themselves at their best or in entirety in the course of a test lasting an hour. This applies both to adults and children. The next objection applies only to children, in whom voluntary control of attention is not developed. It is this. The questions asked in many of the tests are so intrinsically silly, and the tasks which the examinees are set to perform are so dull, that clever children often find it impossible to take them seriously, and all children, dull and clever alike, are unable to feel interest in the tests, and lacking interest, do not trouble to work, or are even positively incapable of working, to the best of their ability. Tests having these defects cannot be expected to yield correct results for every individual tested. Nevertheless, the fact remains that, in spite of the prevailing uncertainty in regard to what, precisely, the tests do test, in spite of their practical shortcomings, the tests have proved themselves up to a point pragmatically valuable. Children who have been graded in schools according to the findings of the intelligence tests have in most cases turned out to be rightly graded. The available statistics seem to show that those who have done well in the tests do generally turn out to be intelligent in the popular sense of the term. The tests work, imperfectly, no doubt, but still as well as may be expected, considering that the technique of testing is still in its infancy.

Assuming, as we must, that there is a real correlation between intelligence and success in the tests, we may now briefly state a few of the statistical results obtained by the testing of large numbers of children and adults. Observation seems to show that human beings reach mental maturity at the age of about sixteen. Further development may take place after this age ; but it is small. The adult differs from the adolescent not in being more intelligent, but in having more and wider experience. The boy's intelligence works on materials offered by a man's memory. Variations in intelligence may be expressed in terms of mental age, or of deviation from a numerically defined normal intelligence. The conception of mental age is chiefly used in cases where children are being tested. Applied to adults, it seems slightly absurd. Still, it is of interest to know that an adult with a mental age of eight can live outside of the asylum and make his living by performing the lowest and most unskilled kind of manual labour. Those with less than half the normal mental age are generally treated as defectives or imbeciles. The wholesale testing of the American army during the war revealed a surprisingly large percentage of adults having a mental age from eleven to thirteen. The test was admittedly rather a rough-and-ready affair ; but the results cannot be completely neglected. The more elaborate tests of Terman in America and Burt in England have shown that intelligence (or at least the correlated capacity to succeed in the tests) is distributed in a very symmetrical way round a numerically determined normal. If 100 be the median point, about 34 per cent. of children (and presumably adults) will be found with mental ratios of between 96 and 105. (A mental ratio is obtained by dividing the child's mental by his chronological age. Thus an eight-year-old who succeeds in tests which can only be passed by the average child of ten will have a ratio of ten over eight, or 125.) Proceeding up the scale, we find 23 per cent. with mental ratios of between 106 and 115 ; 9 per cent. with ratios from 116 to 125 ; 2.3 per cent. with ratios from 126 to 135, and 0.55 per cent. with ratios from 136 to 145. The figures on the opposite sides of the median point are much the same. Twenty per cent. have mental ratios of between 95 and 86, and for the next three lower groups of ten ratios we have the following percentages : 8.6, 2.3, and .33. The lower end of the scale is inadequately represented, because the children examined were children in ordinary schools. The majority of children with mental ratios of 55 and under are educated in special schools for the deficient.

INTELLIGENCE AND UPBRINGING

We have now to consider the horizontal differences between intelligences that are due to environmental causes. Intelligence, as we have seen, is not the same in all individuals of the human species. Men and women are hereditarily endowed with one particular kind of intelligence in exactly the same way as they are hereditarily endowed with eyes and hair of one particular colour and a nose of one particular shape. But at any given period and in any given society or social class there will exist a generally accepted conviction of the intrinsic reasonableness of one particular class of ideas, the validity of one kind of thought-process, the moral rightness of certain types of action, the sacredness of certain institutions and things. This conviction tends to give a special bent to the intelligence of those who entertain it, by setting definite limits to their conception of the Reasonable and the Right, and so confining the activity of their intelligence within a clearly demarcated realm of thought. The mechanism of this process must now be briefly described.

Our most important and deeply rooted convictions are acquired, as might be expected, in childhood and in youth. Children tend to accept what their elders tell them sufficiently often, just as they accept day and night, the wetness of water and the blueness of the sky. The social tradition is regarded by them as a phenomenon of nature, a fixed, unalterable fact. Children form a habit of believing in the ideas generally accepted in the society surrounding them in much the same way as they form a habit of speaking the language of their district and class. Habits of behaviour facilitate activity in one particular direction—canalize it, so to speak, in a certain channel. In the same way habits of thought canalize thinking, scoop out a course along which it must flow, unless more or less violently deviated. Changing the metaphor (it is difficult to speak of mental happenings except in metaphorical terms), we may say that the beliefs which the child or the young person has formed a habit of accepting become in a real sense a part of the mind, conditioning the activity of the intelligence and serving to some extent as its instrument. The earlier a belief has entered into the mind, the more associations it will have collected round itself and the more inextricably will it have become involved with the feelings and instincts. That wonderfully acute psychologist, Cardinal Newman, has described the process with such inimitable clarity that I cannot do better than quote his words. ' An idea under one or other of its aspects grows in the mind by remaining there ; it becomes familiar and distinct, and is viewed in its relations ; it leads to other aspects and these again to others, subtle, recondite, original, according to the character, intellectual and moral, of the individual ; and thus a body of thought is gradually formed, without his recognizing what is going on within him. And all this while, or at least from time to time, external circumstances elicit into formal statement the thoughts which are coming into being in the depths of his mind ; and soon he has to begin to defend them ; and then again a further process must take place of analysing the statements and ascertaining their dependence on one another. And thus he is led to regard as consequences, and to trace to principles, what hitherto he has discerned by a moral perception and adopted on sympathy ; and logic is brought in to arrange and inculcate what no science was employed in gaining.'

ORTHODOXY AND HERESY

The man who will lightly sacrifice a long-formed mental habit is exceptional. The vast majority of human beings dislike and even actually dread all notions with which they are not familiar. Trotter, in his admirable *Instincts of the Herd in Peace and War*, has called them the 'stable-minded,' and has set over against them a minority of 'unstable-minded people,' fond of innovation for its own sake. Here, it may be, we have yet another plane along which the mass of humanity may be divided. The tendency of the stable-minded man, whether he be introvert or extravert, visualizer or non-visualizer, will always be to find that 'whatever is, is right.' Less subject to the habits of thought formed in youth, the unstable-minded naturally take pleasure in all that is new and revolutionary. It is to the unstable-minded that we owe progress in all its forms, as well as all forms of destructive revolution. The stable-minded, by their reluctance to accept change, give to the social structure its durable solidity. There are many more stable- than unstable-minded people in the world (if the proportions were changed we should live in a chaos) ; and at all but very exceptional moments they possess power and wealth more than proportionate to their numbers. Hence it comes

71

about that at their first appearance innovators have generally been persecuted and always derided as fools and madmen. A heretic, according to the admirable definition of Bossuet, is one who ' emits a singular opinion '—that is to say, an opinion of his own, as opposed to one that has been sanctified by general acceptance. That he is a scoundrel goes without saying. He is also an imbecile—a ' dog ' and a ' devil,' in the words of St. Paul, who utters ' profane and vain babblings.' No heretic (and the orthodoxy from which he departs need not necessarily be a religious orthodoxy ; it may be philosophic, ethical, artistic, economic), no emitter of singular opinions, is ever reasonable in the eyes of the stable-minded majority. For the reasonable is the familiar, is that which the stable-minded are in the habit of thinking at the moment when the heretic utters his singular opinion. To use the intelligence in any other than the habitual way is not to use the intelligence ; it is to be irrational, to rave like a madman.

In a society where the current world-view is anthropomorphic, where magic is accepted as a fact, and animistic notions prevail, a man who expresses matter-of-fact materialist opinions about the world will be thought mad, and his type of reason be regarded as unreason. In a different society, where the ideas and methods of physical science have acquired prestige, it is the man with magical and animistic ideas who will be thought unreasonable. In either case, a set of familiar ideas has become axiomatic. The reasoners of each society start from a set of axiomatic major premisses. They think in terms of notions which have become, by long familiarity, the instruments and moulds of their thought and the channels along which all rational thinking must inevitably flow.

Lévy-Bruhl has shown that in almost all primitive societies the ideas of natural death and accident are unknown and practically unthinkable. When a patriarch of ninety dies, it is not of old age, but because some one has desired that he should die and has used magic to kill him, or else because the man himself has done something unlucky or failed to do something lucky. Similarly, if a child falls into a river and is drowned or eaten by a crocodile the event is in no circumstances accidental; it has been willed, perhaps by a human being, perhaps by a spirit. For the primitive, death is invariably murder. To people among whom such notions are axiomatic, are what the rationalists would call 'necessities of thought,' our modern ideas of accident and death from natural and impersonal causes seem utterly unreasonable. And let it be noted that there is no method of conclusively *proving* that we are right and the primitives wrong. If we do not now believe in magic and the activity of invisible beings, it is because we have devised other hypotheses to account for

the phenomena of nature, hypotheses which
have the aesthetic merit of being simpler than
the magical theory of the world and the practical
merit of being to a great extent susceptible of
expression in mathematical terms. The action
of magic cannot be rendered in an equation ;
evil spirits cannot be isolated by chemical
analysis ; but that is no proof that they do
not exist—it is only a proof that the framers of
scientific theories have chosen to leave them
out of account, just as they have chosen to
leave out of account our human attributions of
value. The primitive might admit the existence
of our natural laws, while insisting that we
had forgotten to take account of the magic
and the devils lurking behind the superficially
impersonal phenomena. We reject the devils,
not because we can actually demonstrate their
non-existence, but because they do not fit into
our contemporary world-view, which seems to us
true mainly on pragmatic grounds — because
it enables us to control natural forces. Magic
and devils offend our sense of probabilities
and a certain aesthetic feeling for what is intellectually ' good form.' A study of history
shows that belief in witchcraft was not destroyed
by intellectual argument. (Indeed Glanvill's
argument in favour of the existence of sorcery
was intellectually much more convincing than
any argument adduced against it.) It died
out because educated men had adopted a new

world-view, different from that which had been accepted by the believers in magic. In the world which Galileo invented and Newton brought to perfection there was no room for witches ; they seemed absurd and therefore they ceased to be believed in. For most people living in the West to-day the notion of an impersonal nature is so familiar that it has become axiomatic, a ' necessity of thought.' It is one of the pre-ordained channels along which all ' rational ' thinking must flow. There remains, however, an intransigent minority of natural animists, magicians and mystics, who have the courage to stand out against the popular and, to them, profoundly unreasonable notions of their materialistic contemporaries.

ORIGIN OF PREVAILING PHILOSOPHIES

Translating what has just been said into psychological terms, we can say that in primitive societies the prevailing world-view is, roughly speaking, that of the introvert ; in the contemporary West it is the extraverted attitude to the universe which carries prestige and which, inculcated from earliest youth, is adopted as the natural and necessary attitude by the majority of educated men and women. It may be asked how these two contradictory world-views came successively to dominate a world where the relation of introverts to extra-

verts has remained (it is to be presumed) numerically constant. The question must be answered
in some such way as this. Primitive men, like
the children of to-day (and not the children
only), make an imperfect distinction between
subject and object. If an object inspires emotion, they tend to attribute some of the vital
activity taking place within themselves to the
object which evoked it. What they perceive is
not the external object, but their own emotional,
imaginative, or intellectual reaction to it. This
primitive habit of thought persisted even in
such highly cultivated and intellectual societies
as the mediaeval. It persisted because it was,
after all, an exceedingly natural habit of thought.
If a thing inspires terror, the obvious reaction
is to regard it as a fearful thing. If it feels hot
to the touching finger, if it seems beautiful to
the eye, what more natural than to regard it
as intrinsically hot, and beautiful in itself?
The process of neutralizing objects, of localiz-
ing the emotions and sensations to which they
give rise, exclusively in the perceiving subject,
is one which does not naturally suggest itself
to the average man. It is a step which men
would not have taken unless they had had
good reason to take it. That good reason was
offered them by Galileo and his successors.
By depriving objects of their share in the
spiritual life of man, by leaving to them, as
real intrinsic qualities, only such character-

istics — extension, mass, and duration — as are susceptible of being measured, and once measured, described in mathematical terms, the physicists of the seventeenth and the eighteenth centuries made possible the fabulous developments of modern science. A world regarded from the introvert's view-point, a subjectivized world, with which the observer lives in a state of what Lévy-Bruhl calls '*participation mystique*,' is unamenable to scientific treatment. It may be an exceedingly agreeable and picturesque world to inhabit; but it is not a world for physicists and mathematicians. The scientific theories of the Middle Ages were fruitless theories. Not much could be discovered about the stellar universe by means of that aesthetic astronomy which saw in the 'perfection' of the circle a valid reason for believing in the circular motion of the planets. The qualitative physics of hot and cold, wet and dry, was entirely ineffective when it came to measuring and controlling the world of things. The moralizing natural history of the Bestiaries made charming literature, but it did not tell any one anything of practical value about wild animals. Dame Nature's whimsical abhorrence for vacua might explain the reason why water should rise in a pump (although why the abhorrence should cease after thirty feet or so was always a mystery); it could not explain any of the other phenomena for which we now account by atmospheric

pressure. Galileo invented a world of independent objects, deprived of all the qualities
with which human beings had endowed them,
except the qualities of mensurability. The immense success of science and its consequent
prestige have led to the extravert-scientific
viewpoint being almost universally adopted in
the contemporary West. In their enthusiasm
for scientific materialism, pronounced extraverts attack the problems of the inner life and
attempt to judge them by their own extraverted standards — with results that even to
a fellow-extravert like myself seem utterly
ludicrous. When psychological education is less
rudimentary than it is at present, people belonging to different types will recognize each other's
right to exist. Every man will stick to the
problems, inward or outward, with which
nature has fitted him to deal ; and he will
be restrained, if not by tolerance, at least by
the salutary fear of making a fool of himself,
from trespassing on the territory of minds belonging to another type.

INDIVIDUALS AND THE WORLD-VIEW

At any given moment there is a predominant
world-view. In what way is the congenital
introvert or extravert, as the case may be,
affected by a social tradition whose psychological sign is the opposite of his own ? Will

the inborn tendency be counteracted by the opposite tendency imparted to his mind by education ? Will his nurture, in other words, prove stronger than his nature ? Will nature win the day ? Or will he in some way discover a compromise ? Most frequently, I think, the individual finds a compromise between his inborn and his acquired tendencies. Let us consider the case of an extravert brought up in a society where the prevailing world-view is introverted. The natural orientation of his mind is outwards, towards the object, and there is nothing in what he has learnt to prevent him from giving full play to his outward-tending impulses, provided always that he interprets the objective universe in terms of the introvert world-view. Thus the primitive, when occupied with the practical affairs of life, is whole-heartedly orientated towards the object. In the fabrication of his traps and weapons, his boats, his utensils, his houses, he is as carefully objective as any Western engineer. His arms are the best he can make, his canoe the most perfect that his means and knowledge permit him to build. But if he misses with the first few shots, if he has an accident on his first journey, he will bury the blow-pipe that has taken him weeks to make, he will never use his canoe again. They are inhabited by bad luck. The extravert's objective material world has been interpreted in terms of an introverted world-view. Thus we see that the extraverted primitive will pay the most scrupulous attention to outside objects, will treat them, up to a point, in a completely materialistic and scientific spirit. But if anything unexpected takes place in connection with the objects, anything which he finds disagreeable or not immediately explicable, he reverts at once to the subjective, animistic interpretation of the world current in his society. Things which he had treated materialistically become the home of dangerous and personal powers which must either be propitiated or simply avoided. In the same way, the mediaeval extravert (and there are plenty of mediaeval people living at the present time) tempered a purely matter-of-fact and naturalistic treatment of external objects with acts of superstition designed to conciliate his own personal world-view with that imposed on him by surrounding society. The mediaeval experimentalist could satisfy his craving to make researches into the objective world on condition that the facts discovered were interpreted in terms of the magical, introverted cosmogony imagined by the theologists and philosophers of the period. It must not be supposed that this introverted interpretation of objective facts was made reluctantly by the average mediaeval extravert. Brought up to believe that there was no alternative to the world-view of his epoch, he accepted it as axiomatic.

To interpret the objective facts in terms of it seemed to him almost as natural as had seemed his own spontaneous interest in the facts. It is often difficult for us to distinguish between the second nature that is the product of habit and the hereditary first nature with which we are born.

So much for the compromise by means of which the extravert adjusts his native tendencies to the world-view of an introvertedly-thinking society. In societies like our own, where the world-view is predominantly extraverted, it is the introvert who has to adjust himself by means of an analogous compromise. The mind's internal creations are still regarded by the introvert as possessing more significance, an intenser and more durable reality, than the objects presented to him from without by his senses; but in deference to the current prejudice in favour of objective as opposed to subjective reality, he makes use of external facts to build up his imaginative structure. Introverts who in another age would have used their intelligence to fabricate metaphysical systems and fantastic cosmogonies devote themselves to science, and are distinguished for the creation of fruitful hypotheses. Even the makers of cosmogonies now find it necessary to employ materials quarried from the objective world; the lucubrations of the theosophists and their kind are full of mysterious ' rays,' ' vibrations,' ' ethers,' ' magnetic currents,' and the like.

VITAL INCONSISTENCIES

Many introverts do not make a compromise between their inherited tendencies and those imposed on them from without. They solve the problem of adjustment by living discontinuously. At certain times and in respect to one class of subjects they think in the fashionable extravert style. At other times and in respect to other subjects they think introvertedly, in the manner that comes natural to them. The two systems of thought may flatly contradict one another ; but that, to all but a very few exceptional beings, is a matter of no importance. Men have to live before they think ; and to one who would live efficiently, peace of mind is of vastly greater consequence than logical consistency. If peace of mind can be obtained only by sacrificing logic, then logic goes by the board, not merely unregretted, but unnoticed by its generally quite unconscious sacrificer. I have already quoted in the first of these essays the curious case of Newton the mathematical physicist and Newton the interpreter of prophecy. Many other examples of intellectual inconsistency in men hardly less illustrious might easily be cited. The intellectual inconsistencies of lesser beings are matters of daily and hourly observation. This personal inconsistency is made possible by the inconsistencies in the philosophy of life that prevails at any given time and in any given society. I have spoken in the first of these essays of the way in which the sacredness of a thing or an idea varies according to what may be called its emotional distance from ourselves. The nearer, the more sacred. We may make another generalization and say that the nearer the thing to ourselves, the more likely it is to be thought of in terms of an introverted, subjective philosophy. Objects at a certain emotional distance cease to be treated according to introvert standards and tend to be regarded as mere objects, obedient to other laws than those which govern the human spirit. We have seen that the primitive, living in a society dominated by an introvert philosophy, will treat objects matter-of-factly and naturalistically, until some event occurs which brings them into close emotional proximity to his spiritual being. As soon as the object becomes a source of emotion in himself, he begins to judge it by the standards of his acquired introverted philosophy, and to behave towards it accordingly. In societies dominated by an extraverted philosophy, a matter-of-fact, extraverted attitude towards life is adopted to within quite close emotional proximity to the subject. But when a certain limit is passed, a sudden change is made, and the facts of life are judged by introverted standards. Where man himself is concerned, the current world-view is still

introvert in its character. This attitude of
man towards himself is probably inevitable,
and in the main correct. The spiritual activities of man—his arts, his religion, his love, his
philosophy—cannot finally be judged in terms
of an objective world which they obviously
transcend. The scientifically systematic extravert should be encouraged to push his researches
to their limit, to judge in terms of his extravert philosophy everything that admits of being
so judged. Wherever the material correlations
of a spiritual activity are measurable they
should be measured. But in no circumstances
will an account of these measurable material
correlations constitute a complete explanation
of the spiritual phenomena they accompany.
The introvert will always be justified in offer-
ing other explanations in terms of his subjective philosophy. But such introverted explanations are less justifiable when applied to human
activities, whose scene is, not the inward, but the
outward world. Our social traditions admit the
judgment by introverted standards of political,
economic, juridical, and moral happenings, with
which they are quite incommensurable.

With regard to all that concerns ' nature '
(by which is meant everything in the universe
that is not human), our modern Western education is purely matter-of-fact and extraverted.
The Bestiaries of classical and mediaeval times
have given place to non-moral Natural Histories ;

children are no longer taught that comets portend strange events in the human world, or that thunder is the bellowing of a divinity outraged by the wickedness of man. We are made familiar with matter-of-fact views about nature from childhood, and only those who are congenitally very mystical ever think of regarding them as unreasonable. But where humanity is concerned, education is of an entirely different kind. The child is brought up with strange metaphysical entities, such as Absolute Good, Absolutely Perfect Political and Economic Systems, Pure Reason, Natural Rights, and many other supernatural monsters of the same kind. The result of this state of affairs is only too plainly visible in the modern world. Compared with Western science, Western politics and morals are rudimentary. They are in much the same state as was science when external phenomena were still judged in terms of an introverted philosophy. It is to be hoped that the time will come when those human activities whose scene is the external world will be treated as matter-of-factly as we now treat non-human objects.

VARIETIES IN THE WORLD-VIEW

I have spoken so far as though the prevailing world-view were uniform throughout the whole of a society. But this is not in fact the case.

What an individual learns depends to a certain extent on the class in which he is born and brought up, and the economic conditions in which he passes at any rate the most impressionable years of his life. Those who would interpret all social phenomena in terms of class warfare and the play of economic forces make a great mistake. That the classes into which a society is divided are not homogeneous, that economic interests are not all-powerful, must be obvious to any one possessing the most superficial acquaintance with history. It constantly happens that men of the same class and having the same economic interests take opposite sides in a dispute. Religious, dynastic, and political loyalties are frequently stronger than the loyalties of class and profession. In many other cases, however, an individual's thoughts and actions are undoubtedly conditioned by the class to which he belongs and the economic conditions in which he lives. It is impossible to make a sweeping generalization one way or another. The influence of class and money is neither all-powerful nor negligible.

Before education was made universally compulsory, a difference in class and economic standing often meant a fundamental difference in intellectual upbringing. The poor were not educated at all, with the result that they tended to think in a more primitive and introverted fashion about the world than did those who had been brought up to regard at any rate non-human nature in a matter-of-fact, extra-verted, and more or less scientific manner. This is no longer the case. The whole community is now brought up to accept the extraverted world-view. Difference in class no longer implies, as it once did, a radical difference in world-view. Class and money determine, not the nature of the individual's intelligence, but the way in which it shall be used and the ends which the individual sets himself to attain. Thus, it is sufficiently obvious that intense poverty and continuous exhausting labour prevent any but a very few of the poor and hard-working from using their intelligences in the sphere of abstract thought. An upbringing in commercial surroundings, coupled with the need to earn a living, will predispose a man to set up the making of money as the end of life, and to use all his intelligence to achieve that end. And so on. Any one who possesses the smallest first-hand knowledge of life knows the difficulties which individuals of different classes experience in communicating with one another. Given a common language in which to talk, two men of the same class but belonging to different nationalities will be likely to feel more at ease with one another than two men of the same nationality but of different class.

This last statement, it goes without saying, is true only when the nationalities in question possess the same sort of culture and civilization. Between men belonging to nationalities whose cultures are radically dissimilar mutual understanding is very hard, even when they belong to the same class. The upper-class Englishman and the Rajput noble have a certain fellow-feeling, because they occupy analogous positions in their respective social orders. But they make contact only at a few points. In most of the affairs of life they find themselves separated by the gulf which traditions and education have fixed between them. The Englishman, his thinking conditioned by the extraverted world-view which the West has made its own, confronts (at what a distance!) the Indian product of an introvert philosophy. A man of the twentieth century is trying to communicate with a man of the Middle Ages—and of a Middle Ages, to make matters worse, innocent of Christianity, unacquainted with the classical world of the Mediterranean, brown instead of white, and baked by a tropical sun.

EDUCATION

Education is applied to the mind and to the body. The body is visible, and our ideas about it are in consequence tolerably correct. Nobody imagines, for example, that the right way to nourish the body is to pump food under pressure into the stomach, or that the muscles can be best developed by subjecting them to prolonged, unintermitted, and exhausting strain. Many people, it is true, eat the wrong things in the wrong way, and take inadequate and improper exercise. But that is their own fault. Rational systems of physical education exist, and those who are prepared to submit themselves to such systems have an excellent prospect of keeping their bodies in the highest state of efficiency attainable by each individual. To enable every individual to attain and preserve this maximum efficiency is the aim of all education. It would be foolish to say that the existing systems of physical education have actually achieved this goal. None of them is perfect. But many are at any rate very fairly good, and none is marred by the enormous blunders and stupidities which characterize our systems of mental education. The problem of bodily training has been solved—

89

not completely, indeed, but at any rate to a sufficient extent. We know enough about the matter to avoid making serious mistakes. Our systems are adequate, and we can be tolerably certain that we are on the right road.

Consider now our systems of mental education. About these it is impossible to cherish the same comforting certainty. There is no reason whatever for supposing that the systems current in the West at the present time are those best calculated to raise the individual Western mind to its highest attainable efficiency. Indeed, there are excellent reasons for supposing that they make it entirely impossible for the minds of their victims to develop to the full. Their imperfections make them interesting. Criticism whose object is perfect, or nearly so, is supererogatory. To criticize something imperfect is always amusing, and may be profitable in those cases where the imperfections can be remedied.

I attributed the efficiency of our systems of physical education to the fact that the body is visible. One cannot make very serious mistakes about the nature of a thing one can see and actually handle. Moreover, the results of mistakes are immediately felt by the body as pain. True, men and women will bear the pains of mistaken bodily training if they can be persuaded that to do so is praiseworthy. Witness the vogue which tight lacing, carriage exercise, high collars and stuffy clothes have had in the West ; the vogue of foot-crushing, skull-distortion, slitting and distending of lips and ears, confinement within doors of women, in other parts of the world. But in general pain will be avoided, and pain is the surest symptom of a mistake in physical education. The results of mistakes in the education of the mind are not so promptly and effectively manifested. The distortion of a mind is not painful. A child may grow up into a mental cripple or paralytic without suffering anything worse than boredom and fatigue. The fact is unfortunate. If children suffered agonies from the process of mental distortion at the hands of their pastors, if the stupid and mechanical teaching of German grammar or arithmetic actually made them scream with pain, we should by this time have learned something about right education. Finding themselves liable to prosecution by the Society for the Prevention of Cruelty to Children, bad teachers would soon mend their ways.

THE MIND

We are unable to see the mind, and find it difficult in consequence to understand its nature. That is the main reason why our systems of mental education are so full of mistakes. What is the mind ? The question is, of course, ultimately quite unanswerable. We do not and we cannot know what mind really is. We do not and cannot know, for that matter, what anything really is. Still, we can get along very well for all practical purposes without knowing. We have no conception as to the real nature of electricity ; but we ride in tram cars, we listen in, we make use of klaxons, electric cigar-lighters, and permanent - waving machines. Without knowing anything about the real and intimate nature of mind, we ought to be able to form quite adequate working hypotheses about it— good enough at any rate to serve as foundations for a system of practical education. Most of the hypotheses hitherto propounded have been singularly and strangely inept. It will be as well to consider the most important of these hypotheses ; for they have exercised, and indeed are still exercising, a great and baneful influence on the current systems of education.

It is difficult for us to understand the nature of invisible entities. When we think of something which exists but which we cannot see, we generally do so in terms of visual symbols. Why ? Because our minds happen to work that way. Even when we are discussing music, we talk to a great extent in metaphors borrowed from the visible world. In this case it matters very little ; for we understand music, we know what it is by listening to it. We do not for a moment suppose that tones really have ' colour,' that a sonata, which is an organism in time, is also a ' structure,' a piece of ' architecture ' in space, that high C is really 'higher' than middle C in the sense in which Mont Blanc is higher than the Eiffel Tower. We do not believe these things, because we know, through another sense than sight, what music is. It happens to be convenient for us to talk about this invisible entity in terms that would be appropriate to something seen and existing in space. We know it, and can therefore use these visual metaphors without danger.

It is different with the mind. Like music, mind is invisible ; and when we talk about it, we find it convenient to use symbols, metaphors, and similes borrowed from the spatially extended world of things seen. But the mind is inaudible as well as invisible ; we have no true notions about it to serve as correctives to our rhetoric.

TAKING METAPHORS SERIOUSLY

Men have talked in a loose metaphorical way about 'the contents of the mind,' 'the storehouse of memory,' 'the threshold of consciousness.' Incidents, for them, are 'imprinted on the memory,' and they have 'explored the recesses of their minds' in search of hidden motives or mislaid knowledge. Such phrases and many others as vividly picturesque and no less inaccurate are constantly repeated, until finally those who use them begin to take them seriously and come to regard the mind as though it really were

a sort of house with rooms, or a box divided up
into compartments into which things can be put.
This pretty conceit is systematized and becomes
a scientific hypothesis. The compartments are
labelled, their occupants are given names. There
is a cognitive compartment, where sensations
from the outside world turn into ideas, and having
been transformed, proceed to associate with one
another. (Elaborate and extremely unsatisfactory hypotheses have been propounded by
those who think it peculiarly scientific to explain
mind in terms of matter, to account for the association of ideas by neurone movements in the
brain. They need not delay us here.) There are,
besides the pigeon-hole of the intellect, an affective compartment full of emotions, and a conative compartment in which the will resides. And
of recent years the psycho-analysts have added
a sort of basement, in whose almost unrelieved
darkness the vermin of the unconscious crawl
and pullulate. ' On the threshold,' says Dr.
Freud, ' there stands a personage with the office
of doorkeeper, who examines the various mental
excitations, censors them, and denies them admit-
tance to the reception room (of consciousness)
when he disapproves of them.' The result of
the combined activities of all these sensations,
associating ideas, emotions, conations, censors,
and the like is an individual—is you or I.

Now the mind, whatever the language we
may use to describe it, is obviously not a box

with compartments. The mind, like the body, with which it is associated to form an individual whole, is a living organism, composed of interdependent parts, which we may for convenience of description name and classify as separate entities, but which have no separate existence in reality, apart from the whole to which they belong. The first mistake of the psychologists was to take their own visual metaphors too seriously ; they reduced the living mind to a mere receptacle. The next was to endow their system of classification with a real objective existence. The catalogue has been treated as though it were the reality which it summarily describes. The psychologists have hypostasized, and indeed almost personified, their abstractions. Thus ideas have become independent entities capable of associating with similar ideas, much as birds of the same species mate together in the spring. The Freudian censor is a real person with lodgings inside the skull. The emotions are so many allegorical figures, like the Virtues, Muses, and Deadly Sins in old pictures.

THE MIND AN ORGANISM

The most superficial consideration of the nature of living things should have preserved psychologists from these fallacies. We do not treat the body of an animal as though it were merely the sum of its parts. We do not say, for example, ' I see a tail, and four legs, and a pair of eyes, and two ears, and a lot of teeth and fur, coming down the street.' We say first, ' I see a dog,' and then proceed to classify its parts. The whole organism is the fundamental thing and gives sense to the parts. The parts co-operate to make the whole, are interdependent, and have no significance, cannot even exist, except in relation to the whole organism. If we must use analogies to describe the mind, let us take the analogy of the body. The body is a pattern that persists in spite of a continuous changing of its material ; it is like a fountain which preserves the same shape, although the drops which compose it at one moment are not the same as the drops which compose it at another. Each species of animal has a pattern which is, in some entirely inexplicable way, fore-ordained for it, and every individual of the species comes into existence with a pre-destined pattern of its own, varying in details from the specific norm. When I eat a lettuce, the substance of the leaves is turned into human cells and becomes a part of the individual me. When my pet rabbit eats a lettuce, the leaves become rabbit. The same substance serves in the one case to sustain or enlarge a man-pattern, in the other a rabbit-pattern. Nothing could well be more mysterious.

It is the same with the mind. The mind of an individual is a fore-ordained pattern, varying in detail from the norm of his species. When I look at a lettuce, I integrate my sensations into my own peculiar human mind-pattern. The rabbit looks and absorbs what he sees into a rabbit's mind-pattern. And just as in the absorption of nourishment the whole body is directly or indirectly involved, so too the whole mind in all its aspects, intellectual, affective, conative, is involved in the absorption of experience from the outside world. Ideas do not associate themselves inside the box which is called the mind ; they are associated by a living organism, whose dominating intellectual passion is a passion for meaning and significance. Sensations, however frequently repeated, do not automatically imprint themselves on the memory ; the living organism receives them only if they seem significant, and therefore worthy of attention. The mind is not a receptacle that can be mechanically filled. It is alive and must be nourished. Nourishment is best absorbed by the organism that feeds with appetite. If we treat the stomach as though it were a bucket and pump food into it, it will in all probability reject the nourishment in a paroxysm of nausea. So will the mind.

PSYCHOLOGICAL FACTS AND EDUCATIONAL THEORIES

Bodies have their idiosyncrasies. They vary, not only in size, shape, and strength. but also to some extent in chemical behaviour, in their capacity to absorb certain kinds of nourishment, in their reaction to stimuli. These physical variations, though considerable, are not so great as the variations in the accompanying mind. And for an obvious reason. Man must at all costs survive. A too considerable departure from the physical norm is punished by immediate destruction. The forces of external nature are not so hard on the mind. Provided that he goes on eating and avoiding danger, a man can think how he likes. The mind takes advantage of this leniency on the part of nature. Left free to vary (within limits, of course, which it cannot overstep without bringing itself and the body to destruction), the mind varies—how considerably, and in how many ways, I have tried to show in an earlier essay.

Our educational policy is based on two enormous fallacies. The first is that which regards the intellect as a box inhabited by autonomous ideas, whose numbers can be increased by the simple process of opening the lid of the box and introducing new ideas. The second fallacy is, that all minds are alike and can profit by the same system of training. All official systems of education are systems for pumping the same knowledge by the same methods into radically different minds. Minds being living organisms, not dustbins, irreducibly dissimilar and not uniform, the official systems of education are not, as might be expected, particularly successful. That the hopes of the ardent educationists of the democratic epoch will ever be fulfilled seems extremely doubtful. Great men cannot be made to order by any system of training, however perfect. The most that we can hope to do is to train every individual to realize all his potentialities and become completely himself. But the self of one individual will be Shakespeare's self, the self of another Flecknoe's. The prevailing systems of education not only fail to turn Flecknoes into Shakespeares (no system of education will ever do that) ; they fail to make the best of the Flecknoes. Flecknoe is not given a chance to become even himself. Congenitally a sub-man, he is condemned by education to spend his life as a sub-sub-man.

OUR DEBT TO THE IMBECILES

Before embarking on any speculations about the ideal and possible future systems of education, it is necessary to give some account of the existing system and of the reforms in it which have already been made.

It is to the imbeciles and the mentally deficient that we owe such reforms as have been made in the old systems of education. If the mind is a mere receptacle which can be filled mechanically, as one fills a jug with water, it follows that a child who does not learn remains ignorant only through lack of good will ; he deliberately closes his mental box, he refuses, malignantly, to admit the knowledge which his teachers are trying to pump into it. There is only one remedy : he must be compelled to open his mind ; the opposing will must be broken— by moral persuasion, by threats, by physical torture. The fine old system of mechanical repetitive teaching, tempered by flagellation, was developed and perfected through the centuries.

No systematic effort was made in the past to teach the mentally deficient. They were left in the full enjoyment of their imbecility. The more eccentric lunacies received medical treatment, which consisted of a combination of imprisonment, starving, and beating. This system was designed to drive out the devils, by whom our Bible-reading ancestors imagined all madmen to be possessed. With the growth of that strange new spirit which we call humanitarianism there arose a new sense of responsibility towards these unfortunate beings. Efforts were made to lift them out of their imbecility, to educate them up towards normality. As soon as this effort was seriously made, it became manifest that the current methods of educating normal children were entirely inadequate and unsuitable when applied to deficients. It was obvious that, if imbeciles could not learn, it was not through any malignant refusal to admit knowledge ; it was through inability. They could not be flogged into opening the doors of their mental boxes, they could not be bullied into learning uninteresting things by rote ; but they could, it was gradually found, be persuaded, be stimulated and amused into acquiring some kinds of knowledge. They remained deficients ; but at least they were now deficients who had been educated up to the limits of their native capacity.

Imbeciles are not different in kind from normal folk, only in degree. Between the idiot and the man of exceptional ability stretches an unbroken series of graded types. The method of teaching which is found suitable for the lowest type will be suitable—with proper modifications—for the highest. If the best way of teaching deficients is to interest them in what they have to learn, then that is also the best way of teaching the normally and abnormally intelligent. It pays to treat the minds of idiots as though they were delicate living organisms requiring careful nurture ; it does not pay to teach mechanically, even when such teaching is backed by threats and flagellation. Imbeciles cannot learn, even after countless repetitions, the things which do not interest them. The same applies to more intelligent children. True, they are intelligent enough to learn something, even when the teaching is dull, mechanically repetitive, and brutal. But they would learn more if they were taught by the same methods (*mutatis mutandis*) as have proved successful in the training of imbeciles.

The helplessness of very small children, their incapacity to think and will as adults do, are almost as manifest as the helplessness and incapacity of deficients. Indeed, a deficient may be regarded as one whose mind has never grown up, so that when his chronological and corporeal age is, shall we say, ten years, his mental age is only two. The methods of teaching this abnormal child of ten will therefore be entirely suitable when applied to the normal child of two. The obvious resemblance of the deficient to the infantile mind has led to great reforms in the organized teaching of small children. The education of infants in Kindergartens, Montessori Schools, or Macmillan Nursery Schools compares favourably with even the best systems of training devised for larger children. To the systems of mechanical education current in our ordinary schools it is incomparably superior. Where the official systems ignore psychological facts, infant education, as developed in the best modern schools, is realistically scientific. Where they create misery, boredom, an insubordination requiring rigorous repression, and a hatred of learning, it spreads joy, self-discipline, and the eager desire for knowledge.

EDUCATION

There are many kinds of infant schools ; but
all are conducted on fundamentally the same
principles. The aim of all of them is to teach
the child to teach himself. First of all, the
senses are trained. Playing, the child is given
practice in seeing, hearing, touching, smelling.
This training of the senses is of the highest
importance. Sensuous impressions are the basis
of all mental processes ; the more things we
have touched, seen, heard, the richer will be
our imagination, the more we shall have to
think about, and the greater the number of
ways in which we shall be able to think. Further,
the process of exercising the senses stimulates
the whole infantile mind, strengthens it and
quickens its growth. Imbecile children given
exercise in the handling of objects have developed
and improved. Left to themselves or to the
mercy of untrained parents—whose love is
only equalled by their total ignorance and in-
eptitude in the matter of education—children
receive a most inadequate sensuous training,
especially if brought up in the drab and sordid
environment of a city. The systematic training
of the senses is of vital importance to every
town-bred child.

Sensuous training is combined with hand-
work, which at this early age is necessarily of
the simplest and most rudimentary kind. Much

ingenious apparatus has been devised for the child to train his fingers on. But learning to dress is in itself an education—a better one, perhaps, than learning to do things with much more elaborate and far-fetched apparatus than laces and buttons. For clothes are near and important to the child, and it is through that which is immediately significant to the learner that all education should begin. Few adults and practically no children are interested in abstract things, or, for that matter, in anything outside the circle of their immediate experience. To teach a number of ' subjects,' entirely unrelated to their daily lives, is to guarantee for your pupils inevitable boredom, a difficult learning, and an all too easy forgetting. Children should learn as the human race learned ; they should set out from the immediate and the concrete to discover the abstract, the general, and the remote. History and geography should begin with the family and the native place. The sciences must blossom out of the local flowers, must be born with the familiar animals, spring from the neighbouring rocks and waters, be deduced from the practice of the local crafts and industries. Geometry must arise as it arose among the Egyptians—from the measurement for practical purposes of definite individual spaces. Arithmetic must solve the actual problems of daily life. And so on. Higher education is so remote from ordinary life that it hardly affects the majority of learners. Most of our contemporary Babbitts have been to the university. A higher education that turns out such products must indeed be in need of reform. The interests, the intellectual outlook, of the educated Babbitt are exactly the same as those of the uneducated. This means only one thing : the various ' subjects ' taught at our educational establishments are so completely disconnected with life that it never even occurs to the learners to absorb them into the practical workaday part of their minds ; it never even strikes them that knowledge may be used to enrich ordinary experience, to test prejudices and conventions of conduct. Philosophy, science, literature are so many ' subjects,' learned and forgotten. The essential Babbitt remains unmodified by them. He emerges from the university the unregenerate Philistine he was before he entered. If knowledge is to be loved for its own sake, if it is to affect the conduct of the generality of mankind (as it is essential in this rapidly changing modern world that it should), it is necessary —for most adults and adolescents as well as for all children—that what is now abstract and remote should be wedded in some way to practical life, that it should be made to spring from the ordinary experiences of modern man, and so be enabled to modify his conduct.

In the best infant schools this synthesis of knowledge and practical life is an accomplished fact. An analogous synthesis of the vastly more complicated knowledge imparted in the course of higher education and the practical interests of adolescents and adults must be made. The need is urgent. If we go on as we are doing now, we shall not merely fail to profit by the immense accumulations of knowledge which a few eccentric historical researchers and men of science have piled up ; we shall carry our civilization headlong to disaster. A twentieth-century material civilization cannot be worked by people whose minds are predominantly mediaeval or even prehistoric.

The training of the imagination follows and accompanies the later stages of the sensuous training of small children. Children are encouraged to make things for themselves, to act, to make believe, to tell stories. The powers of self-expression are strengthened by this practice ; the child learns confidence in himself. Moreover, the teacher takes care to direct the children's play into educational channels. She sees to it that the children's games of make-believe take the form of pretending to be prehistoric men, Romans, ancient Britons — it is a history lesson. Playing with mud and sticks and water, they make islands, lakes, mountains, rivers ; they are learning geography. They are told and then re-tell, act over, stories from fable and history. Speaking and acting dissipate shyness, give control of the voice and gestures, and enable the children, by actually living their literature, to understand it to the full. The reading of Shakespeare forms a part of the ordinary curriculum of English-speaking school children. Read in the ordinary way by a class of children sitting at desks, out of a horrid little school edition provided with the sort of notes that one can be examined on, a play by Shakespeare seems meaningless and dull. Naturally ; Shakespeare did not write his plays to be read, with notes, by children sitting at desks ; he wrote them to be acted. Children who have read the plays dramatically, who have lived through them with their whole imaginative being, acquire an understanding of Shakespeare, a feeling for the poetry, denied to those who have ploughed through them in class and passed, even with honours, an examination in the notes.

No teacher of small children should attempt too early to teach anything requiring sustained flights of abstract logical reasoning. In the vast majority of children the logical faculty develops late ; small children, like savages, do not admit the cogency of logic. The powers of ratiocination should be exercised in following trains of argument, which must be progressively lengthened, as the feeling for logic grows, from the shortest possible piece of pure reasoning to the longest each pupil is able to follow. And in all cases, as we have seen, these exercises in pure ratiocination should start from the near, concrete, and therefore interesting fact.

THE OFFICIAL SYSTEM COMES INTO ACTION

From the infant school (if he has had the luck to be sent to one instead of being brought up by incompetent parents or nurses) the child must pass to an elementary or preparatory school. The change is, in almost every case, profoundly for the worse. The methods of instruction current at a good infant school are psychologically sound. At the ordinary boys' or girls' school the education is founded on a psychological fallacy, and the child is too often regarded as existing for the System, not the System for the child. At this school and at others exactly resembling it in spirit and in educational methods the child must remain until the time comes for him—if it ever does come—to go to the university. There, if he has the luck to go to the right kind of university, he will once more be receiving education of a reasonable and decent sort. He may, on the contrary, go to a bad university, in which most of the vices of the unreformed schools are stupidly perpetuated. In that case, he will go out into the world without ever having known, except during a few years of early childhood, what a proper education is. The astonishing thing is that he contrives to learn as much as he does. That he could, if taught in the right way, be made into a much better and more intelligent citizen than he becomes under the present system, one cannot doubt. But it may be remarked parenthetically that the absurd and irrational systems of education under which they were brought up have not in the past prevented men and women of outstanding talent from fully developing their powers. In spite of no education, in spite of what is worse, mechanical and brutal education, they have been themselves, they have done their work. They were too strong for their environment : they educated themselves. Ordinary folk succumb to their environment. They suffer themselves to be taught (which is all that most educationists want them to do), and so become what the system makes them, dim, incurious people, not desiring knowledge, and quite ignorant of the way in which knowledge may be obtained if it should ever be needed. What is required is a system of education which shall encourage boys and girls (not merely infants, as is at present the case) to teach themselves ; a system calculated to foster the child's curiosity through all the years of growth, to make the desire for knowledge a chronic and habitual desire, and to familiarize each child with the best methods of acquiring it by his own efforts. What is needed, in a word, is a system of individual education.

Let us briefly trace the career of the growing school child. In the infant school, if he was lucky enough to attend one, he was taught to teach himself, to develop his own faculties, to use his senses and his imagination — the herald, as Goethe called it, and indeed the parent of his reason. His education was an active one. In the higher schools, to which he is now promoted, the education is mainly passive. No longer is he expected to use initiative, to discover things for himself. His first duty is now to sit still and let the school master or mistress teach him. He is regarded as an empty vessel. The function of the teacher is to fill him. In the infant school, on the contrary, he was regarded as a living, developing organism, and the teacher was there to create an appetite in him for knowledge and virtue, to make truth, beauty, and goodness tempting, and to show him the best way of acquiring these things by his own efforts. A great gulf separates the two schools.

In the higher schools the child finds himself a member of a class — of a very large class in most schools, except those of the rich. (And even in these — I am thinking in particular of the English Public Schools — the classes are sometimes fantastically large.) There may be forty, fifty, even sixty children with him in the same room. His talents are expected to conform to the average standard of this assemblage. He may be exceptionally clever and quick, or exceptionally slow and dull. In either case he is a nuisance to his teacher and to his fellow pupils, and in either case his own education suffers. If he is clever, he is held back by the majority of ordinary boys. If he is stupid, he is dragged along so fast that it is impossible for him to learn anything completely and thoroughly. Passively, with his forty or fifty dissimilar and unique companions, he sits at his desk while the teacher pumps and mechanically re-pumps information into his mental receptacle.

> Ram it in, ram it in!
> Children's heads are hollow.
> Ram it in, ram it in!
> Still there's more to follow.

If the teacher is a severe disciplinarian, the child will sit still and at any rate appear to drink in his words. If the teacher is lax, he will more frankly day-dream, scribble, fidget, openly play the fool. Satan, we know on good authority, finds work for idle hands to do. While the teacher is discoursing, the child is necessarily idle, passive, unoccupied. Moreover, the lesson is generally dull and has to be constantly repeated, owing to the incapacity of a young mind to fix its attention on anything that does not interest it. Each repetition makes the lesson slightly duller. Even the work which

the children have to do for themselves—sums,
translations, answers to questions referring to
the last history or geography lesson, and
so on — cannot truly be called occupation.
For such tasks are too often no more than
meaningless exercises, unrelated to anything in
the child's experience and performed for their
own silly sake, because the teacher has said
that they must be performed, without interest
or desire. In how different a spirit will a
child undertake a task, even the most arduous,
which he feels to be significant and important !
Plunged in such work — work he can really
see the sense of—he will be really and truly
occupied. Satan will find no extra work of
mischief for him to do, and the question of discipline will simply not arise. But of this later.

THE DANGERS OF GOOD TEACHING

Hitherto we have been considering the uninspired teacher, who works his or her way dully
and mechanically through the prescribed curriculum. But teachers may be, and frequently
are, charming, intelligent, and persuasive. They
may put things well ; they may speak in a
way that will command attention and awake
emotion and enthusiasm ; they may have a
power of making difficulties seem easy. The
child will listen to such teachers and will greatly
appreciate them — particularly if he has an

examination to pass in the near future. But
the more accomplished a teacher is in the art
of lecturing or coaching, the worse he is as an
educator. Working on the old-fashioned system,
the clever teacher (deplorable paradox !) does
almost more harm than the stupid one. For
the clever schoolmaster makes things too easy
for his pupils ; he relieves them of the necessity
of finding out things for themselves. By dint of
brilliant teaching he succeeds in almost eliminat-
ing the learning process. He knows how to fill
his pupils with ready-made knowledge, which
they inevitably forget (since it is not *their* knowledge and cost them nothing to acquire) as
soon as the examination for which it was required is safely passed. The stupid teacher, on
the other hand, may be so completely intoler-
able that the child will perhaps be driven,
despairingly and in mere self-defence, to educate himself ; in which case the incompetent
shepherd will have done, all unwittingly, a
great service to his charge, by forcing him into
a rebellious intellectual independence.

MASS EDUCATION

The defects of the ordinary system of mass
education are so enormous that it is hardly
necessary to expatiate on them any further.
They may be briefly summarized as follows.
First, the system of teaching in large classes is

intolerant and rigid. No allowance is made for the idiosyncrasies of the individual child, who is sacrificed to the average of the class. The class and the fixed curriculum are like the bed of Procrustes in the myth ; those who are too long for the bed are cut down until they fit ; those who are too short are stretched. The child who is quick and talented in one subject but not in others (and every human being has his special gifts) is compelled under the current system of mass education to sacrifice his talents to his deficiencies. Thus a child may have a great talent for English and none for arithmetic. He may be endowed with a real feeling for literature, a gift of composition ; but when you ask him what percentage of a floor 18.7 feet long by $51\frac{3}{16}$ metres wide remains uncovered when you have spent three pounds eleven shillings and sevenpence three farthings plus 26 rupees 12 annas on linoleum costing $279.06 per acre, he finds it difficult or impossible to reply. He must therefore remain in a low class, where they read nothing but baby books and concentrate on spelling and grammar, until such time as he can solve this interesting and instructive problem.

Second, under the present system of mass education by classes too much stress is laid on teaching and too little on active learning. The child is not encouraged to discover things on his own account. He learns to rely on outside help, not on his own powers, thus losing intellectual independence and all capacity to judge for himself. The over-taught child is the father of the newspaper-reading, advertisement-believing, propaganda-swallowing, demagogue-led man —the man who makes modern democracy the farce it is. Moreover, lessons in class leave him mainly unoccupied, and therefore bored. He has to be coerced into learning what does not interest him, and the information acquired mechanically and reluctantly, by dint of brute repetition, is rapidly forgotten.

Third, the child, being bored and unoccupied, is also mischievous. A strict external discipline becomes necessary, unless there is to be chaos and pandemonium. The child learns to obey, not to control himself. He loses moral as well as intellectual independence.

Such are the main defects in the current system of mass education. Many others could be mentioned ; but they are defects in detail and can be classified under one or other of the three main categories of defects—sacrifice of the individual to the system, psychologically unsound methods of teaching, and irrational methods of imposing discipline. We need a new system of universal education of the same kind as that which has proved itself so successful in the training of defectives and infants, but modified so as to be suitable for older boys and girls. We need, as I have said in an earlier paragraph, a system of individual education.

INDIVIDUAL EDUCATION

Nearly every one, I suppose, will admit in principle that education ought to be basically individual. The objections of those who oppose educational reform along individual lines are mainly practical objections. 'Mass education,' they admit, 'has its defects. But it is the only reasonably cheap and workable system that can be applied to the training of large numbers of children. Individual education must always be reserved for the fortunate few who can afford to pay for an expensive privilege.' Of recent years, however, these practical objectors have been proved wrong. A working teacher has devised a system of individual education which can be applied to large numbers of even the poorest pupils, which costs no more than the old system of class teaching, and which has triumphantly stood the test of practice. That system, devised by Miss Parkhurst and named, after the American High School in which it was first applied, 'the Dalton Plan,' has been worked with great success during the past four or five years in a steadily increasing number of elementary and secondary schools in England; has returned with increased prestige to the land of its origin, where it is beginning to be widely appreciated ; has been worked successfully in India, China, and Japan ; and is engaging the attention of educators in most of the countries of continental Europe. True, the number of schools in which the Dalton Plan is being worked in its entirety is still very small. But there are many in which it has been partially applied, and still more where its influence has tempered, if only a little, the prevailing spirit of mass education. All the signs are encouraging, and we may hope that the movement inaugurated by Miss Parkhurst will have profound and far-reaching effects on the educational practice of the whole world.

The Dalton Plan has been expounded in theory and described in action by a number of educationists, notably Miss Parkhurst herself and Mr. A. J. Lynch, the Headmaster of a Daltonized Elementary School in North London. Their books deserve to be read by all who take an interest in the training of children. I can do no more here than summarize what they have to say, adding a few personal impressions of a visit to a Daltonized school.

The first step in the Daltonization of a school consists in the abolition of class rooms and the substitution of specialist rooms. School rooms, used under the old system for the accommodation of specified classes at specified hours, become subject laboratories to which the children go — more or less as the spirit moves them in the course of the school day—to do their work for themselves. Each child knows exactly what he has to do ; for he is provided with an assignment of work covering a whole year and divided up into shorter periods of months and weeks. At the beginning of each month he sees how much work is to be covered in the course of the twenty school days which it contains, and he is given for his guidance an estimate of the amount of time in which an average child may be expected to get through each item of the whole assignment. The child, of course, will not exactly adhere to this schedule ; nor is it desired that he should—the whole object of the Dalton Plan being to permit each child to work in his own way and at his own speed. But it is advisable to give the children an idea of the average time required for the work, so that they may have a standard by which to judge of their own performance and the relative importance of the subjects.

Let us imagine a child arriving one morning at his Daltonized school. He feels that he would like to start the day, shall we say, with geography. He makes his way (after the usual formalities of roll call) to the Geography Room or Laboratory, where he takes his place with the other children who have had the same idea as himself. A teacher who has chosen to specialize in geography presides over the room, and it is to him or to her that the child comes for advice in difficulties, and for the correction of his written work. (The Dalton Plan, it may here be remarked, calls for the production of a great deal of written work ; the teachers have a heavy burden of corrections ; but the pupils are well exercised in the art of lucid and logical expression.) The teacher is careful, when the child appeals to him for advice, not to make things too easy for his pupil ; he is not there to 'coach,' to hand out lumps of ready-made knowledge, to give recipes for the successful passing of examinations ; he is there to show the child how to teach himself. He confines his help, wherever possible, to telling the child how and where he can find the information which will solve his difficulties. For this purpose every specialist room is provided with a small but efficient reference library of the subject in question. The children are encouraged to use this library, and are shown how to profit by indices and bibliographies. The result is, that they soon become adept research workers, knowing exactly how to set about finding whatever piece of information they require. To my mind, this is one of the most valuable secondary results of the Dalton Plan. I have often had occasion to be amazed at the helplessness of even quite well educated people to correct their own ignorance, even when they earnestly desired to do so. Confronted with some specific problem, they have been utterly without a notion of how to set about finding the solution. Libraries surround them ; but they do not know how to use them. Catalogues, bibliographies, subject indices are mysteries to them. Brought up in schools where the teachers gave them the finished products of research and neglected to show them how to conduct researches of their own, they are wholly at a loss when they have to teach themselves. The child whose education has been on the Dalton Plan goes out into the world equipped with all the technique of the research worker. If he desires to continue his own education he knows the best way of doing so. He need waste no time or energy doing the wrong things.

But it is time to return to our child in the geography room. We left him doing the work specified for him in his assignment. He will do it either by himself or in consultation with friends — one of a co-operating group of children, of whom each contributes something to the general store. The silence of the old class room is abolished, and with it the preposterous notion (based on the evil system of competition and mark-grubbing) that it is dishonourable and punishably criminal to give help to or be helped by one's fellows. When he has accomplished his particular job, or when he is tired of the subject and feels in need of a change, he takes his work to the presiding specialist for correction, has the amount done (if done satisfactorily) checked up in his individual work- and time-chart, and announces his intention of moving on to the History, the English Literature, the Arithmetic Room, whichever it may be. The master looks at the child's work-chart, and if he sees in it no manifest and cogent objection agrees, and the child goes off to the subject laboratory he has chosen. Taking his place (if he finds room), he goes on with his assignment of work at the point where he left off at the end of his last visit to the room. If the master finds, on consulting his chart, that the child is very much behindhand in one particular subject, he will probably advise him on leaving the Geography Room to work at the weak subject rather than at any other. Mr. Lynch found it advisable to institute a special Adjustment Room, in which children who were abnormally weak in any subject could go and get special help of a kind which it would have been impossible to give in the crowded subject rooms.

It must not be thought that Daltonians disapprove entirely and on principle of class teaching. Certain subjects, they have found (notably arithmetic), are best taught by a combination of class with individual work. They attach due importance to the inspirational teaching of masters or mistresses, who can use their prestige and personality to create in a whole class of pupils an enthusiasm which will serve to heighten the children's zeal for individual work. They appreciate the value of class teaching when it becomes necessary to sketch the outlines of a whole subject, or to explain a general principle to a number of children of about the same capacity. And they assemble classes—or perhaps it would be more accurate to call them 'conferences'—of boys and girls for the double purpose of thrashing out difficulties and exercising the powers of correct speech and rapid, impromptu reasoning. In practice, at most Dalton Schools, the periods of individual work are alternated with briefer class periods, which serve to vary the tasks, prevent monotony, and relieve the fatigue which, it has been found experimentally with children, results from an uninterrupted process of self-education.

MERITS OF THE DALTON PLAN

First among the merits of the Dalton Plan must be counted the emancipation of the individual from the system—the substitution of an elastic educational scheme for the rigid bed of Procrustes, to fit whose unalterable length the victims of the old methods were stretched or brutally lopped. Under the Dalton scheme every child works at the speed and in the way most suitable to his individual idiosyncrasies. The naturally quick do their work quickly. An exceptional child will get through the year's assignment in eight or nine months. There is no waiting for promotion ; as soon as he has finished one year's work he proceeds to the next. Thus a talented English Elementary schoolboy leaving school at fourteen may actually —if he is at a Daltonized school—be doing the work of an average Secondary school-boy of fifteen and a half or sixteen. In the old schools this talented child would have had to mark time in every class while he waited for the end of the year for his promotion ; in the highest class he might very likely have had to repeat the same year's work twice over. That would have been his punishment for not being ordinary.

The slow boy will perhaps take eighteen or even twenty-four months to accomplish a year's work. But he will accomplish it thoroughly, he will have mastered every word. Under the old system he was hurried along uncompre-hending at the heels of his quicker class-mates. Slow workers are not necessarily stupid, and the examination records of slow children trained under the Dalton Plan are surprisingly good.

To the individual peculiarly gifted in one direction but not in others the Dalton Plan offers an opportunity of showing his mettle. True, official examinations being what they are, children may not neglect the subjects in which they are congenitally incapable of attaining proficiency. But at least the Dalton Plan gives them a better chance than did the old system of understanding the subjects for which they are poorly endowed, and expressing themselves to the full in those for which they have a natural gift.

The second great advantage of the Dalton Plan is that the child learns, and is not taught, either mechanically or well. A certain percentage of children, as of grown-ups, are naturally lazy and will not work. (These, when asked their opinion of the Dalton Plan, express an unqualified dislike for it. Daltonism, they complain, makes one work ; under the old system one could doze away half one's time.) The majority of girls and boys, however, really enjoy doing work which is interesting in itself or which, even if it is not interesting in itself (as much work necessary for the attainment of proficiency in a difficult subject inevitably must be), belongs to an interesting class of studies, and is realized as important. In Daltonized schools children are taught the art of teaching themselves. They learn by their own efforts, and therefore remember what they learn in a way which is impossible to children who accept ready-made knowledge from their teachers, or learn mechanically by dint of mere repetition.

The effect of the Dalton Plan on the morale of the schools where it is worked is no less remarkable than its effect on the minds of the children.

In a well-run Daltonized school the problem of discipline solves itself. The children, being all occupied and interested, have neither the time nor the desire to be mischievous. I had read a good deal about the Dalton Plan ; but it was only recently that I paid a visit to a fully Daltonized school ; and though in theory and from books I knew what to expect, I must confess that I was astonished by what I saw. The school which I visited (the West Green School, whose Headmaster, Mr. A. J. Lynch, is the author of the excellent books already referred to) is an Elementary School in an all but slummy district of North London. Most of the boys bore the obvious stigmata of poverty, and came from the class of homes in which it is least easy to give children a desirable training in manners and general behaviour. Yet I have rarely if ever seen a set of small boys whose ways I liked better. They behaved themselves—incredible as it may sound !—like rational human beings. Their manners were good, but easy ; their attitude to strangers courteous and independent. They obeyed the masters, but entirely without servility or fear ; it was evident that in this school the teachers had come to be regarded as friends and helpers, not as enemies. The good order and industry of the school rooms was not incompatible with quiet discussion among the boys and the occasional passing of pupils from one room to another. When the bell rang for the mid-morning recess, the boys went on behaving like rational human beings. They put away their books, they got up quietly, they walked out without noise. Mentally I contrasted this behaviour with that of the severely drilled and repressed children of an ordinary school class. I thought of the strained, unnatural silence before the pealing of the bell, and then of the wild, demoniac whooping, the Gadarene rush and scramble as soon as the master's tyranny is relaxed and the signal for release is given. It was the contrast between the recreation of free, rational, responsible beings and the wild Saturnalia of slaves.

LIBERAL EDUCATION

How children are taught has been the subject of the preceding sections. It is time to consider what they are taught. The democratic ideal has been that every child should be given a complete Liberal Education, that is to say, an education in the humanities, literature, pure science, languages, and mathematics. The theory of the Liberal Education must be briefly summarized. It is supposed that youths who have been taught the grammar of various dead and living languages, who have learned a certain amount of mathematics and natural science, who have read extracts from the best authors and practised the art of composition, will be thereby fitted to solve all the problems and deal with all the emergencies of practical life. A Liberal Education prepares young people for life by training their intellects. A man who has received a Liberal Education may be trusted to think well and quickly in any crisis. His mind has been strengthened by wrestling with philological and mathematical difficulties, just as his body might be strengthened by doing gymnastics. A liberally educated man, if he should ever find it necessary to learn some new and unfamiliar subject, will do so with ease, because his mind has been invigorated and trained to use its strength in the best and most economical way. In other words, ability acquired in academic studies is transferred to other activities. Such is the theory at the back of Liberal Education.

Being easily grasped and specious, it is not surprising that this theory should have been long and tenderly cherished. The question naturally arises : How far does it correspond with the facts ? The answer is, that it does correspond to some extent, but not so completely as was once supposed. Ability in one subject is transferred to another only in certain circumstances. The child who has been taught, say, classics or elementary mathematics in such a way that he understands what he is learning, in such a way that he realizes the subject as a whole and is made to feel that it is worth the trouble of learning, is likely to transfer the ability acquired in this subject to other subjects. The boy who, on the other hand, has been drilled and bullied into a certain proficiency in the classics or in arithmetic will not transfer his acquired ability to other subjects. I cannot do better in this connection than quote the words of Mr. Charles Fox, whose admirable *Educational Psychology* deserves to be read by all who desire to think clearly and accurately about the subject of education. ' A review of the evidence already presented,' writes Mr. Fox, ' leads us to realize that the whole problem of the effects of training must be viewed from a different angle. We must turn from the sphere of psychology to the realm of ends. For, if immediate results are aimed at without considering the ultimate aim of education, it is possible to acquire a high degree of particular skill without affecting general capacity. Where, on the other hand, an ideal is consciously pursued, a motive is at work which is capable of changing the whole mental outlook, since it is of the nature of an ideal to engender a " divine discontent " with whatever falls short of it. To revert to our original example, a training in mathematics may produce exactness of thought in other departments of intellectual work, and a love of truth, provided that the training is of such a kind as to inculcate an ideal which the pupil values and strives to attain.' Given

intelligent teaching of a kind which interests
and seems of value to the pupil, ability can be
transferred from one subject to another and
the intensive study of one subject may be a real
mental gymnastic, exercising and strengthen-
ing the intellect. That is rather different from
the idea so fondly cherished by our fathers :
that a child who had been bullied into mechanically learning Latin grammar, or any
other equally uninteresting and insignificant subject, has received a complete mental training,
and is capable of reasoning rapidly and cor-
rectly about any problem which may present
itself.

Ability can be transferred only in those cases
in which the child has been interested in the
subjects he has been taught, and can regard
them as genuinely important. The chief defect
of the curriculum of a Liberal Education is
that the majority of children are not interested
in academic subjects, and are unable to see
that they have any significance whatsoever
outside the class room and examination hall.
I cannot speak from personal experience in
this matter because, as it happens, I have the
kind of mind to which an academic training
is thoroughly acceptable. Congenitally an intellectual, with a taste for ideas and an aversion
from practical activities, I was always quite
at home among the academic shades. Liberal
Education was designed for people with minds

like mine. But in the course of my sojourn among the academic shades, how many people I have met to whom the whole business seemed only a tiresome joke ! Either they neglected their studies altogether ; or if they were compelled by economic pressure to be industrious, they plodded away with bored and weary industry until the examinations were safely over, consoling themselves meanwhile with anticipations of a time when they would never have to open a serious book again. All teachers agree that the majority of pupils in secondary schools, and even in universities, belong to this class ; they are simply not interested in the subjects that are taught, they are bored by the prevailingly abstract method of teaching. A Liberal Education in the eyes of these students is merely a liberal, even a prodigal, waste of time. Democratic states finance this waste of time to the tune of many millions annually. In the interests of the individual learner as well as of social efficiency the existing system requires to be changed.

The first step towards reform must be the recognition that all human minds are not the same, that intelligence differs not only in degree, but to some extent also in kind. From this it follows that no single curriculum is suitable for all pupils. The existing system of academic education may be preserved for the relatively few young people whose minds work abstractly and who are interested in knowledge and ideas for their own sakes. For the less intelligent students of the same type a simplified form of Liberal Education with some definitely vocational bias might be invented. Neither of these curricula would be suitable for the many practical - minded boys and girls, to whom theory is uninteresting and abstraction meaningless. For the more intelligent of these a Liberal Education might be supplied in terms, so to speak, of practice ; they would learn something of science through applied science. The less intelligent of the practically minded would take a similar but less liberal course. Daltonized teaching would in all cases give scope to every pupil to display whatever peculiar talents he possessed. The sorting and grading of pupils would be made on the basis of intelligence tests and the reports of teachers, which would also determine the fitness of pupils to receive advanced school or university education.

UNIVERSITIES

Universities exist for a double purpose—to give advanced specialized training in such subjects as medicine, law, and engineering, for the practitioners of which a high degree of technical knowledge is indispensable ; and in the second place, to encourage disinterested researches and to impart to those capable of receiving it advanced learning of a less obviously and immediately practical kind. A certain proportion of the young people attending universities do so for the purpose of making a career in one of the professions. The rest are there, nominally, to finish their education by the acquisition of disinterested higher learning. In reality, however, most of them attend the university for reasons entirely unconnected with this higher learning, for which they feel no natural appetite and whose nature, significance, and object they are therefore unable to comprehend. They enrol themselves as students, or are enrolled by their solicitous parents, because, in the first place, to have attended a university (particularly if the university happens to be a notoriously expensive one) gives a certain social *cachet* ; because a university is a delightful club for young people ; and finally, because the modern university, at any rate in England and America, is a great athletic organization. When we have deducted from the total number of non-professional students all those who attend the university only for reasons of snobbery and sociability, and for love of sport, the residue of genuine philomaths will be remarkably small. And yet, leaving the professionals out of account for the moment, it is precisely for the philomaths that universities ought to cater. Students who are merely clubmen, snobs, and athletes should be excluded.

Of all the universities, Oxford and Cambridge contain the largest proportion of non-professional and merely snobbish and athletic students. But they make up for this offence by having by far the best system of teaching. It is possible at Oxford or Cambridge to obtain a degree without ever attending any lectures at all. (I myself never attended more than, at the outside, two lectures a week.) These ancient seats of learning were Daltonized long before Daltonism was invented. One is not passively taught at Oxford or Cambridge ; one is encouraged actively to acquire knowledge. At most other universities an entirely disproportionate importance is attached to lectures. Students are compelled to attend innumerable courses, and it is made difficult, often impossible, for a man—however intelligent or well informed—to obtain a degree who has not attended these courses, and is therefore unable to reproduce, parrot-fashion, the favourite ideas and phrases of the lecturing professor. Lecturing as a method of instruction dates from classical and mediaeval times, before the invention of printing. When books were worth their weight in gold, professors had to lecture. Cheap printing has radically changed the situation which produced the lecturer of antiquity. And yet—preposterous anomaly !—the lecturer survives and even flourishes. In all the universities of Europe his voice still drones and

brays just as it droned and brayed in the days
of Duns Scotus and Thomas Aquinas. Lec-
turers are as much an anachronism as bad
drains or tallow candles ; it is high time they
were got rid of.

To encourage research is, as I have said, one
of the functions of a university. Contemporary
universities have been taking this part of their
duties too seriously. They have encouraged research, not only in those cases where research
was worth making, but on all sorts of entirely
unprofitable subjects as well. Scientific research is probably never completely valueless.
However silly and insignificant it may seem,
however mechanical and unintelligent the
labours of the researchers, there is always a
chance that the results may be of value to the
investigator of talent, who can use the facts
collected for him by uninspired but industrious
researchers as the basis of some fruitful generalization. But where research is not original,
but consists in the mere rearrangement of existing materials, where its object is not scientific,
but literary or historical, then there is a risk of
the whole business becoming merely futile. Few
things are so depressing as the average literary
thesis. It deals almost always with some humanly
insignificant fact or person. Inevitably : for all
the significant facts and people have been
written about ; the candidate for post-graduate
honours is compelled to choose the insignificant.

Having chosen his futile subject, he proceeds to treat it with an entirely misplaced scientific methodicalness. If the whole business were not so stupidly boring, one would laugh. For the scientific student of literature is one of the most comical figures of our day. He is as ludicrous in his way as were the literary students of science who flourished during the Middle Ages. We laugh at the men who wrote of the moral significance of elephants and the mystical virtues of triangles ; the men who take infinite pains to reproduce the misprints of worthless authors, to unbury the most trivial facts about perfectly uninteresting people, to discover influences and catalogue borrowings, are no less ridiculous. Indeed, I should say that their activities were intrinsically a good deal sillier than those of the mediaeval exponents of literary science. The mediaevalists sometimes made pleasant literature out of their bogus science, gave utterance occasionally to interesting thoughts. The modern scientific literary researchers produce nothing but boring trivialities. Their only justification is the fact that universities give them Doctorates for their pains, and that Doctorates in the academic world have a higher cash value than mere Masterships of Arts. If universities ceased to bestow these degrees (which testify only to the industry and the absence, in the holders, of all sense of proportion or of humour) the ' scientific ' literary researcher would more or less completely disappear, and the prestige of higher learning, on which his activities bring a deserved discredit, would immediately rise.

THE IDEAL SYSTEMS OF THE FUTURE

So much for education as it is now and as it is likely to become in the immediate future—for its defects are so manifest that it will almost certainly not be allowed to persist in its present form for many years more. In the light of what is, we may imagine what ought to be. In a world like ours—and one must assume that the psychological facts will remain what they are and have been for the last few thousand years — the ideal educational system is one which accurately measures the capacities of each individual and fits him, by means of specially adapted training, to perform those functions which he is naturally adapted to perform. A perfect education is one which trains up every human being to fit into the place he or she is to occupy in the social hierarchy, but without, in the process, destroying his or her individuality. How far it is possible for any one in a modern, highly organized society of specialists to be, in Rousseau's phrase, both a man and a citizen is doubtful. Present-day education and present-day social arrangements put a premium on the citizen and immolate the man. In modern conditions human beings come to be identified with their socially valuable abilities. The existence of the rest of the personality is either ignored or, if admitted, admitted only to be deplored, repressed, or, if repression fails, surreptitiously pandered to. On all those human tendencies which do not make for good citizenship, morality and social tradition pronounce a sentence of banishment. Three-quarters of the man is outlawed. The outlaw lives rebelliously and takes strange revenges. When men are brought up to be citizens and nothing else, they become, first imperfect men and then unsatisfactory citizens. The insistence on the socially valuable qualities of the personality, to the exclusion of all the others, finally defeats its own ends. The contemporary restlessness, dissatisfaction, and uncertainty of purpose bear witness to the truth of this. We have tried to make men good citizens of highly organized industrial states : we have only succeeded in producing a crop of specialists, whose dissatisfaction at not being allowed to be complete men makes them extremely bad citizens. There is every reason to suppose that the world will become even more completely technicized, even more elaborately regimented, than it is at present ; that ever higher and higher degrees of specialization will be required from individual men and women. The problem of reconciling the claims of the man and the citizen will become increasingly acute. The solution of that problem will be one of the principal tasks of future education. Whether it will succeed, whether success is even possible, only the event can decide.

POLITICAL DEMOCRACY

THE DEMOCRATIC CREED

Mr. Chesterton has been eloquent, among so many other things, about democracy. And since his eloquence is also a lucid profession of the faith that is in political democrats, I shall brighten a page with a rather long quotation from his admirable *Orthodoxy*. 'This is the first principle of democracy,' writes Mr. Chesterton : ' that the essential things in men are the things they hold in common, not the things they hold separately. And the second principle is merely this : that the political instinct or desire is one of these things which they hold in common. Falling in love is more poetical than dropping into poetry. The democratic contention is that government (helping to rule the tribe) is a thing like falling in love, and not a thing like dropping into poetry. It is not something analogous to playing the church organ, painting on vellum, discovering the North Pole, looping the loop, being Astronomer Royal, and so on. For these things we do not wish a man to do at all, unless he does them well. It is, on the contrary, a thing analogous to writing one's own love letters or blowing one's own nose. These things we want a man to do for himself even if he does them badly.

I am not here arguing the truth of any of these conceptions; I know that some moderns are asking to have their wives chosen by scientists, and they may soon be asking, for all I know, to have their noses blown by nurses. I merely say that mankind does recognize these universal human functions, and that democracy classes government among them. In short, the democratic faith is this, that the most terribly important things must be left to ordinary men themselves—the mating of the sexes, the rearing of the young, the laws of the state. This is democracy; and in this I have always believed.'

There is something very engaging about Mr. Chesterton's mixture of frankness and sophistry. He professes a chronic and unshakable faith in conceptions which he admits are quite probably not true. 'I am not here arguing about the truth of any of these conceptions,' he says, with an honesty which does him enormous credit. But he then goes on to confuse the issue by talking about vicariously chosen wives and delegated nose-blowing. We are led by this rhetorical device to discount the previous admission. So few people want their wives chosen and their noses blown by some one else, that their existence may be ignored. The implication is that we may also safely ignore the existence of the equally small number of people who do not want to do their own governing. The truth is, of course, that the people who do not want to choose their own wives or blow their own noses are infinitely rarer than the people who do not want to take a share in ' ruling the tribe.' Mr. Chesterton began admitting the fact, but changed his mind half-way and decided to mitigate the frankness of his confession. He had begun to say something like this : ' I think that all men *ought* to take an interest in government, and I think so passionately in spite of the fact that, in practice, most of them take no interest whatever in the matter.' But since a frank and full statement of the fact would have made nonsense of his political ideal—for a statesman's notion of what ought to be is merely silly and academic if it does not stand in some sort of living relationship with what is—he checked himself half-way, and having admitted that his ideal might not necessarily rhyme with the facts, proceeded to imply that, after all, it did rhyme more or less.

THE DEMOCRATIC FACTS

All observation, however, tends to show that this particular conception of what ought to be has very little connection with the things that are. Men ought, no doubt, to take an interest in law-making and the rule of the nation. (And here let me remark parenthetically that Mr. Chesterton's use of the word ' tribe ' instead of 'nation' was another ingenious and artistic trick ; for 'tribe' connotes a small agglomeration of human beings, 'nation' a large one. Plenty of people, as I shall show later, are interested in the local or vocational politics that affect their daily lives. And they are not only interested in them ; they are well qualified to handle these small problems successfully. But few, on the contrary, are interested in national and international politics ; and fewer still are qualified to cope with the major problems of statesmanship. By using the word 'tribe,' Mr. Chesterton evoked the cosy and idyllic atmosphere of the Greek or mediaeval city-state, of the Indian wigwam and the palaeolithic cave. 'Nation' would have summoned up all the enormously complicated and uncomfortable realities of modern industrial life. Mr. Chesterton is an artist in words ; it is a pleasure to draw attention to his artistry.) Men ought, I repeat, to take an interest in law-making. But in point of fact they seem, at ordinary times, to take very little interest. A considerable proportion of voters never vote at all. My morning paper informs me very opportunely that at the Brixton bye-election (27th June 1927) only 53 per cent. of the electorate voted. In this borough nearly half the men and women who ought to have been helping to rule the tribe were so little interested in the process that they could not trouble to walk to a polling booth. So much for the non-voters. And out of every hundred of those who do use their privilege at election time, how many take a consistent and intelligent interest in politics in the unexciting interval? If we compare the numbers of voters enrolled as members of the various political parties with the total number of voters on the registers, we shall be able to form some idea of the ratio of politically interested to politically uninterested people. It will be found that the uninterested are in an enormous majority. It is almost inevitable that this should be so, for it is a matter of common observation that few men, and vastly fewer women, are interested in things which do not immediately affect their daily lives. Whenever government becomes so intolerably bad that it seriously affects the interests of each individual, when it oppressively robs men of the comfort, the prosperity, the personal privileges to which they have been brought up to think themselves entitled, people tend to take a passionate interest in law-making. The standard of governmental oppressiveness varies from age to age with the standard of living and the ideas of inherent rights and privileges current among the oppressed. The contemporary French peasant would revolt against any government which attempted to do a hundredth part of the things which were done as a matter of course under the *ancien régime*. His standard of living is so much higher than that of his ancestors, he takes for granted as natural and inalienable so many rights and privileges of which they never dreamed, that for him a government is oppressive when it acts in ways which his fathers would have regarded, not merely as not particularly oppressive, but even as actually humane. In different societies governments reach the oppression-point at different times ; but when the point is reached, the reaction, in the shape of intense political interest, is always the same. When the particular grievances which brought dissatisfaction to a head have been remedied, the sustained interest in politics dies down, and as long as the rulers govern in such a way that the ruled do not feel themselves adversely affected personally by their activities, so long as circumstances remain normally propitious (for political unrest may be aroused by accidents over which the rulers have no control, and for which they are in no way responsible), the interest will remain in abeyance.

Interest being proportionate to the distance of the object from the individual, we should naturally expect to find a generally keener interest in local than in national politics. The facts seem at first sight to disprove the general rule. For municipal elections rouse less excitement than general elections ; the number of people who use their local vote is much smaller than the number of those who use their national vote. This seems paradoxical, but in fact is not. For to the inhabitants of a town the local politics need not necessarily be nearer, in the psychological sense, than the affairs of the nation as a whole. If the municipal administration is tolerably efficient, there is no reason why men and women should be in any way personally conscious of municipal politics. Nor is there any artificial agency for creating the interest which is naturally lacking. For newspapers which are always clamorously urging their readers to take an interest in national politics have little or nothing to say about local politics. Much nearer than municipal politics, as distance is measured psychologically, are the politics of vocation. A man may live all his life in a town without ever once being made personally and intimately aware of its politics. But he can hardly fail to be aware of the politics of his trade or profession. Half, at least, of the hours of his waking life are passed at work, and the whole of his material interests are determined by it. National and municipal politics may easily, by reason of their psychological remoteness, be matters of indifference; but not vocational politics. The major vocational problems are also national and international problems. Feeling that these problems are close to him, the average man is interested in them, and to this extent is interested in lawmaking on the grand scale. The granting of a constitution to India was an act intrinsically quite as important as the withdrawal of the Coal Trade subsidy ; but for every man interested in the first piece of statesmanship there were a hundred interested in the second. India is a long way off in space, and for those who have never been there it is more distant psychologically than the moon. The moon, at any rate, has a decided effect upon lovemaking and melancholy meditation ; but there is no reason why India should ever touch us at all.

I have been at some pains to show that, whatever they theoretically ought to do, most men are not in fact much interested in politics which do not directly and obviously affect their everyday lives. This was necessary, because it is impossible to criticize a political ideal without knowing the reality to which it refers. For example, the ideal that men should share their possessions is one in which many people have enthusiastically believed. Judged by religious and transcendental-ethical criteria, it may be an excellent idea. The earliest Christians seem, for a short time at any rate, to have been practising communists. Covetousness and selfishness are vices. These facts are regarded by some people as valid reasons for believing in communism. Not, however, by politicians ; for they are facts that tell us nothing about the political, as opposed to the religious and transcendental-ethical, values of the ideal. Its political value can only be assessed when we know how the majority of human beings feel about private property. If we observe that as a matter of fact most men and women are passionately interested in private property, we shall not regard the idea as politically very sound. And our conviction of its political unsoundness will be confirmed if we find that the practical applications of the ideal have not been successful. Mr. Chesterton's democratic faith, that the making of laws must be left to ordinary men themselves, must be judged, in so far as it is a political ideal, in the same way. We must discover, first, whether ordinary men are interested in making laws ; and in the second place, whether their participation in the government of states has in fact been successful. If they are not interested in ruling the tribe, and if there their efforts to do so have not in practice ' worked,' then we are justified in supposing that the ideal in which Mr. Chesterton believes is not, politically speaking, a sound ideal.

POLITICAL DEMOCRACY IN PRACTICE

The first of these questions has already been answered. Ordinary men, we have seen, are not much interested in any political problems which do not immediately affect themselves.

147

Let us consider, very briefly, the second question, which may be re-stated succinctly thus : Has political democracy worked, does it work now, and is it likely to go on working in the future ? That the lot of ordinary men has been enormously ameliorated in the period during which political democracy has been in practice might seem, at a first glance, to constitute an unequivocally affirmative answer. But a little reflection is enough to convince one that it does not. Political democracy and the amelioration of the common lot are not connected in any necessary way. It is perfectly possible for an autocracy or an oligarchy to be humane, and for a democratically organized government to be oppressive. The common man's lot happens to have been improved during the democratic era, and the improvement has been to a great extent directly due to democracy. We may be duly grateful to democracy without allowing our gratitude to blind us to its defects, and without forgetting that the process of amelioration can be continued under other and politically more satisfactory systems. Not only can it be continued, but, as I shall try to show later, it must be continued—must, that is to say, if the existing system is to be succeeded by a more rational mode of government. The condition, alas, need not necessarily be fulfilled.

The defects of political democracy as a system of government are so obvious, and have so

148

often been catalogued, that I need not do more than summarize them here. Political democracy has been blamed because it leads to inefficiency and weakness of rule, because it permits the least desirable men to obtain power, because it encourages corruption. The inefficiency and weakness of political democracy are most apparent in moments of crisis, when decisions have to be rapidly made and acted upon. To ascertain and tabulate the wishes of many millions of electors in a few hours is a physical impossibility. It follows, therefore, that in a crisis one of two things must happen : either the governors decide and present the accomplished fact of their decision to the electors—in which case the whole principle of political democracy will have been treated with the contempt which in critical circumstances it deserves ; or else the people are consulted and time is lost, with often fatal consequences. During the War all the belligerents adopted the first course. Political democracy was everywhere temporarily abolished. A system of government which requires to be abolished every time a danger presents itself can hardly be described as a perfect system.

The chronic, as opposed to the occasional, weakness of a democratic system of government seems to be proportionate to the degree of its democratization. The most powerful and stable democratic states are those in which the principles of democracy have been least logically and consistently applied. The weakest are the most democratic. Thus a parliament elected under a scheme of proportional representation is a truly democratic parliament. But it is also, in most cases, an instrument not of rule but of anarchy. Proportional representation guarantees that all shades of opinion shall be represented in the assembly. It is the ideal of democracy fulfilled. Unfortunately the multiplication of small groups within the parliament makes the formation of a stable and powerful government impossible. In proportionally elected assemblies governments must generally rely on a composite majority. They have to buy the support of small groups with the more or less corrupt distribution of favours, and as they can never give enough, they are liable to be defeated at any moment. Proportional representation in Italy led through anarchy to fascism. It has caused great practical difficulties in Belgium, and threatens now to do the same in Ireland. Stable democratic governments are found in countries where minorities, however large, are unrepresented, and where no candidate who does not belong to one of the great parties has the slightest chance of being elected. Parliaments in such countries are not in the least representative of the people. They are thoroughly undemocratic. But they possess one great merit which makes up for all their defects :

they can form governments strong enough to govern.

Government of whatever kind is superior to anarchy. We must be thankful for a system which gives us stable government, even when, as happens only too frequently in democratic countries, the men who direct the government are charlatans and rogues. Fate has afflicted the nations with many disastrous monarchs. Hereditary tyrants have often been born imbeciles and bred up to be spendthrifts or criminals. We may feel sincerely sorry for people who through no fault of their own have found themselves saddled with a Nero, a King John, a Kaiser William the Second. But for those who of their own free will elect a Bottomley as their parliamentary representative, a Big Bill Thompson as their mayor (not once, but, in spite of the first disastrous experience, a second time), one can feel less sympathy. The most monstrous rulers have certainly been hereditary despots, not the elected representatives of the people. But we must remember that the history of democracy has been a short one compared with that of despotism. In a century and a half even autocracy could produce few first-rate tyrants. Moreover, the democratic ruler comes to power relatively later in life, and so has had less chances of being corrupt. (The facility with which youths can be corrupted by the premature possession of power or wealth constitutes one of the main arguments against the hereditary principle in government.) It would be surprising if democracy had produced a crop of Neros ; for Neros must be made as well as born, and democracy gives little scope for their manufacture. But though democracy can boast no Nero—only a Robespierre or two and some Djerzhinskys—it has produced a whole Newgate Calendar of lesser ruffians. The history of corruption in all democratic countries, particularly America, is full of heroes. And as for the charlatans and the criminal incompetents —their name is all but legion. This is only to be expected, since the talents required to win public favour are quite different from those which a ruler ought to possess. Demagogues succeed for the same reason as confidence tricksters—because they have a gift of the gab, charm, and an intuitive knowledge of human nature, because their personality is magnetic, and their manner open and affable. Men and women are so suggestible, so easily gulled, that a talented swindler can always be certain of making a handsome living. How much more certain of success is a demagogue ! For demagogues do not ask their victims to give them a wad of banknotes ; they only ask for votes. You can buy things with banknotes, voting papers are worth nothing. Every one is prepared to be generous with his vote. The best democratic leaders have either, by a coincidence,

possessed both the swindler's and the statesman's talents, or else have risen to power by
undemocratic means. Disraeli was a great
political genius who happened also to be a
great demagogue. Lord Salisbury was also an
excellent statesman ; but he would never have
become prime minister in a democratically
organized country if he had not been Robert
Arthur Talbot Gascoyne-Cecil and a Third
Marquess.

Demagogues are not the only or even the
most efficient exploiters of human suggestibility.
The newspaper proprietors have carried the art
of the, confidence trickster to a yet higher pitch.
The spread of elementary education has been
accompanied by a great increase in the influence
of the press. Who reads may run—in the same
direction as his newspaper. This is a fact of
which the rich were not slow to take advantage.
Practically speaking, the whole English press
is now in the hands of four or five rich men.
Plutocratic oligarchs, they aspire to rule, under
cover of democratic institutions, impersonally
and without responsibility. To exploit democracy, they have seen, is easier and more profitable than to oppose it. Let the many vote, but
as the opulent few who own the newspapers tell
them. The many obey — generally, but not
always. Elections may be won, as was demonstrated by the Liberals in 1906, by the Labour
Party in 1923, in the teeth of an almost unani-

mously hostile press. The newspaper proprietors will not rule undisputedly until they have discovered in what circumstances men assent, and in what others they respond to suggestion by deliberate contradiction. They have already realized (what schoolmasters have discovered long ago) that indirect suggestion is less liable to arouse contradiction than direct. Doctored news convinces much more effectually than many dogmatic leading articles. But the science of journalistic confidence trickery is still in its infancy. A time will doubtless come when the propagandist methods of contemporary newspaper owners will seem barbarically crude and inept.

The third main objection to political democracy is that it encourages corruption. The evidence for democratic corruption is written so large over recent American and European history that it is unnecessary for me to catalogue specific instances. I shall confine myself to a few general reflections. Men are afflicted with the original sin of their anti-social instincts, which remain more or less uniform throughout the ages. The tendency towards corruption is implanted in human nature from the first. Some men have strength enough to resist the tendency, others have not. There has been corruption under every system of government. Corruption under the democratic system is not worse, in the individual cases, than corruption under autocracy. There is merely more of it, for the simple reason that where government is popular, more people have an opportunity for acting corruptly at the expense of the state than in countries where government is autocratic. In autocratically organized states the loot of government is shared among a few. In democratic states there are many more claimants, who can only be satisfied with a much greater total quantity of loot than was necessary to satisfy the aristocratic few. Experience has shown that democratic government is generally much more expensive than government by the few.

THE IDEAL IN THE LIGHT OF REALITY

It is now time to reconsider Mr. Chesterton's ideal. Ordinary men, he says, ought to take part in government. But in fact they are not much interested in law-making, while the systems of government which invite them to take part in ruling the tribe are far from satisfactory. Can we, in the light of these facts, go on believing in Mr. Chesterton's ideal? Mr. Chesterton has tried to anticipate criticism by saying that ordinary men ought to govern, even though they do it badly. It was in the same spirit that a Filippino leader recently declared that home rule for the Philippines was desirable, even though it meant 'making hell' of the islands. Once more we can only appeal to the historical reality. Have men in fact enjoyed being governed badly, even when they themselves took part in the government? Have they felt comfortable in hell, even when the hell was of their own making? The answer, surely, is that they have not. Whenever government, even self-government, has reached a certain stage of inefficiency, men have invariably welcomed even a despot, provided that he could give them law and order. Falling in love, says Mr. Chesterton, is more poetical than dropping into poetry, and governing is, or ought to be, like falling in love. But if one wants to read poetry, one would rather read the poetry of Keats than that of an ordinary love-sick young man. Even the ordinary young man himself, however much he enjoys falling in love, prefers Keats's poetry to his own. It is the same 'with government. Helping to rule the tribe may be a very poetical act in itself (though few people seem to find it so) ; but the act has results, and the results may be as bad, in their practical way, as the love-sick young man's verses. History shows that men prefer the political harmonies of the statesman of genius to their own ineffectual or disastrous efforts at ruling. The finished and perfected poetry of good rule seems to them more valuable than the very indifferently poetical act of helping to govern badly.

The passionate quality of Mr. Chesterton's

faith in political democracy seems to be explained by the fact that he can see no alternative to inefficient government by the people except corrupt government by the rich. I share his mistrust of the rich, and believe so firmly in the truth of that distressing saying about the camel and the needle's eye that I should feel exceedingly uncomfortable if some capricious fate were suddenly to make me a millionaire. If plutocracy were indeed the only alternative to inefficient democracy, I should certainly be a good deal less anxious to change the existing state of affairs. But wealth is not the only source of power, nor men's only qualification to rule. There is also, after all, intelligence. Mr. Chesterton finds something poetical about the idea of the ordinary man governing badly ; he approves of the system which invites him to do his worst with the ship of state. Personally I find the idea of being governed well (I myself lack all capacity or ambition to govern) much more poetical ; and I should be in favour of any system which secured intelligent men with a talent for government to do the ruling.

ARISTOCRACY

The creation and maintenance of a ruling aristocracy of mind would not in any degree endanger the cause of humanitarianism. Indeed it would be necessary, in an aristocratically governed state, to carry humanitarianism much further than it has been carried in the democratic state. In a country where it is a principle that the naturally best men should be at the top, careers must be wide open to the talents, and the material conditions of life must be, for all, the most propitious that can be designed. For the naturally best man is so rare that one cannot afford to let him be stunted by an unfavourable environment, or kept down by lack of opportunity. A state that is aristocratic in the etymological sense of the term—a state, that is to say, which is ruled by the best of its citizens—must be socially much more democratic than any state which we know at present. In the contemporary democratic state it is possible for the worst to govern and for the best, if they happen to be born in unfavourable surroundings, to be distorted by disease and hunger, handicapped mentally by inadequate education, and wasted throughout an entire lifetime on unsuitable work. True aristocracy can only exist where there are no hereditary advantages other than those of talent, and where the rich cannot claim to rule on the mere ground that they are rich. It is obviously very unlikely that any of those now living will ever see a genuinely aristocratic state. Indeed, the genuinely aristocratic state may be an actually unrealizable ideal. But it is at least an unrealizable ideal which may be approached in practice without involving in insoluble difficulties those who try to apply it. For it is an ideal which takes into account the unalterable realities of human nature. There are other finally unrealizable ideals which do not take the facts of life into consideration, and which consequently plunge into immediate difficulties all who act in accordance with them. Mr. Chesterton's democratic ideal is an ideal of the second kind. Finally unrealizable, it also leads to immediate trouble when applied in practice. The aristocratic ideal may be equally unrealizable (though even this is not certain) ; but since it is based on an acceptance of the facts, its gradual application to politics cannot be attended by serious difficulties.

The ideal of aristocracy is already acted upon in so many spheres of our social life that its application to all the spheres, including that of government, ought not to be a matter of insuperable difficulty. It is the unfamiliar that men dislike ; the already familiar idea can be developed without arousing any violent terror or rage. The aristocratic ideal—the ideal that the naturally best men should be at the top—is already extremely familiar. In commerce and industry promotion is regarded as the reward of superior capacity. The higher posts are still, it is true, mainly filled by men with hereditary or financial influence. But as economic pressure increases, influential incompetence tends

to be squeezed out, while the men with ability
are forced up from below to take their places.
In the lower ranks influence counts less and the
ideal of aristocracy is consistently acted upon.
The professions are genuinely aristocratic institutions. Doctors and lawyers, engineers and
architects, are only permitted to practise if they
have shown themselves competent to pass a test
of ability. Tests no less stringent are applied
to candidates for official posts under the government. This last fact is particularly significant.
Even in the most democratic countries civil
servants are expected to show some symptom
of exceptional ability. They must be mentally
aristocratic—to the extent, at any rate, of being
able to pass an examination. (That the existing system of examinations excludes some of
the best men is notorious ; but that it also
excludes most of the worst is no less indubitable.
This is a matter to which I shall return at a
later stage.)

Our modern governments, then, are anomal-
ous. On their administrative side they are
definitely aristocratic. Nobody may be a civil
servant who has not passed a test of capacity.
But any one may vote provided he is twenty-
one years old. (In France it has been decided
in a court of law that certified idiots have a
right to vote.) And any one who is not actually
a criminal may stand for parliament, and so be
qualified to become a cabinet minister. This

is a manifestly absurd state of affairs. The men who administer the laws have to give proof of ability and knowledge : the men who make the laws need give proof of nothing at all except the confidence trickster's ability to talk persuasively, or, lacking that, the possession of money or some sort of influence. And yet to make the laws is at least as difficult as to administer them. Indeed, it is much more difficult ; for while the administrator deals with only one kind of law referring to one class of social activities, the law-maker has to consider laws on every subject, and is responsible for all the policies, national and international, industrial, commercial, economic, of a whole country. A man who proposes to become a first-class clerk in a government department is required to prove himself intelligent and well educated. How much more intelligent, how much better educated, should be the member of parliament who makes the laws that are administered, not in one, but in all the departments ! In actual fact, however, an average member of parliament is less intelligent and incomparably worse educated than the average higher-grade civil servant. This, I know, is a sweeping generalization : but any one who has a wide acquaintance among both classes of men will find the truth of it confirmed by daily observation. I have met members of parliament who, whatever their wealth or their powers of tub-thumping might have been, would quite certainly have been unable to enter even the lower grades of the civil service or to work their way in commerce above the rank of copying-clerk.

It would be possible, without making any radical changes in the existing system, to improve the quality of the legislative assembly, simply by demanding from the legislator the same proofs of competence as are demanded from every administrator. If nobody were allowed to stand for parliament who had not shown himself at least capable of entering the higher grades of the civil service, parliament would automatically be purged of many of its worst incompetents and charlatans. It is possible that if this test were imposed a few men of real merit might be excluded, but their loss would be compensated by the exclusion of so many merely talkative and merely rich or influential people, so many ignorant quacks and rogues. If at the same time the right to vote were made contingent on the ability to pass a fairly stiff intelligence test—if nobody were allowed to participate in the government of the country who was not mentally at least fifteen years old—it is probable that the influence of demagogues and newspapers would be considerably reduced. Adults are more judicious, less easily suggestible, than children.

That only mental grown-ups should vote, and that nobody should be allowed to make laws who is not at least as intelligent and well informed as the men who administer them—these are political principles which ordinary common sense must approve. Only the most mystically fervent democrats, who regard voting as a kind of religious act, and who hear the voice of God in that of the People, can have any reason to desire to perpetuate a system whereby confidence tricksters, rich men, and quacks may be given power by the votes of an electorate composed in a great part of mental Peter Pans, whose childishness renders them peculiarly susceptible to the blandishments of demagogues and the tirelessly repeated suggestions of the rich men's newspapers. The principle which makes right and privileges dependent on capacity is so well established in almost every sphere of human activity that the idea of applying it to the organization of government cannot be regarded as strange and revolutionary. Not merely common sense, but even social tradition, can be enlisted on the side of reforms that seek to establish government by grown-ups and men of tested ability for the present chaotic and haphazard system.

These simple reforms would not, it is obvious, transform political democracy at one stroke into aristocracy. They would constitute at most a first step in the right direction—towards government by those best fitted to govern. As things are at present, we do not even make an effort to have ourselves ruled by the most fit; we simply leave the whole matter to chance. Sometimes a few good men appear among the riff-raff of law-makers, sometimes the riff-raff is unadulterated. Fate chooses; we do not. But even if we ardently desired to select the best men, we should not know how to make the selection with anything like accuracy or certainty. The existing tests of ability are certainly better than nothing; but they are still crude and inadequate.

EXAMINATIONS

Much has been said, and with reason, against examinations: that they are tests of mere memory rather than of constructive ability, and that the ability they do test (when they succeed in testing it) is an abstract and un-practical ability, a sort of ghostly pure intelligence existing apart in the academic void. Both these objections are well founded. The first is being met in practice by the gradual transformation of the old-fashioned examination into the modern intelligence test, in the widest sense of that word. Pure parrot memory is coming to be less and less esteemed. The man who knows the text-book by heart unintelligently is not so sure of coming out of the examination with honours as he once was. The time is not far off when he will occupy at the foot of the examination-results list the same lowly position as he is destined to fill in the real unacademic world of thought and action. The other defect of examinations—that they test intelligence in isolation, abstracted from the personality as a whole—is more serious than the first, and is not so easily remedied. It is sufficiently obvious that written answers to a series of specific questions do not provide any basis for a rational judgment of the whole personality. To know a person's character you must at least have talked with him, and unless you are gifted with remarkable intuitive insight you are not likely to know much about him unless you have seen him living and acting over a considerable period of time. The ordinary examination tests only intelligence. That is why it has been found necessary, when selecting candidates for professions in which certain moral as well as intellectual qualities are indispensable, to supplement the written examination by other tests varying in thoroughness from the personal interview to the long-drawn novitiate of the sailor, the military engineer, the priest. The ideal examination of the future will consist of a series of tests designed systematically to gauge the character in all its aspects. The results of such an examination would serve as the basis for an accurate judgment of each individual examinee : in the light of them it would be possible to assign to every man and woman the

PROPER STUDIES

place in the social hierarchy which he or she
was best fitted to occupy.

FITS AND MISFITS

That every human being should be in his
place—this is the ideal of the aristocratic as
opposed to the democratic state. It is not merely
a question of the organization of government,
but of the organization of the whole of society.
In society as it is organized at present enormous
numbers of men and women are performing
functions which they are not naturally suited to
perform. The misplacement of parts in the
social machine leads to friction and consequent
waste of power ; in the case of the individuals
concerned it leads to many varieties of suffering. The man of poor ability who is set to perform a function too difficult for him not only
does the work badly, thereby diminishing the
total efficiency of the society in which he lives, but
himself personally suffers (if external pressure
or his own conscience compels him to take his
work seriously) from a chronic anxiety and
sense of strain, which may and frequently do
result in physical breakdown. The man of good
ability doing work that is too easy for him is
also diminishing the total efficiency of society,
by wasting the major portion of his powers. The
consciousness of this waste of powers breeds
discontent, bitterness, and a kind of cynicism

most disagreeable to the individual himself, and very dangerous to the society in which he lives. The misfit which has the gravest consequences is that of the man deficient in the qualities of leadership who is set over his fellows. Men in authority who nag at their subordinates ; who are malignant or unjust ; who are blinded by their own emotional reactions to the extent of not being able to grasp the objective reality of the event which roused their feelings : leaders who do not know their underlings' jobs ; who are vain and take themselves too seriously ; who lack a sense of humour and intelligence— all these can inflict enormous sufferings on the men and women over whom they are set. And they are responsible not only for suffering but for discontent, anger, rebellion, to say nothing of inefficiency. For it is notorious that a bad commander, whether of troops or of workmen, of clerks in an office or children in a school, gets less work out of his subordinates and of worse quality than a good commander. The misfit of bad leadership is one of the major causes of individual unhappiness and social inefficiency. It is a cause which some suitable system of psychological testing could completely eliminate.

VARIETIES OF EXCELLENCE

These considerations of leadership bring us back to the problem of government. In an

aristocratic state the best must govern. But
the best must not all be the same ; they must
have different excellences. The man who can
deal personally and directly with men is by
no means necessarily the most intelligent ; he
may be able to lead, but incapable of deciding
which way to lead. Conversely, the judicious
maker of plans may be unable to persuade his
fellows to act on his plans. The demagogue
is a low type of leader who can persuade men
to follow him, but cannot distinguish a good
road from a bad road. At the opposite pole
we have the consummate politician who knows
exactly which road to take, but lacks the powers
of command. Sometimes the two types are
united in a single man, and a Napoleon, a Bis-
marck, or a Lincoln makes his astounding and
disquieting appearance. These geniuses of
politics are no less rare than the great men of
science or art. There is no relying on their
emergence. If they appear, they appear : and
all calculations are upset, all prophecies falsified.
But they appear only occasionally, and in the
intervals the world must rely on smaller talents.
Since, as we have seen, it often happens that
the talent of leadership is divorced from that of
political judgment, it will be necessary in the
aristocratic state to make systematic use of both
kinds of excellence. Leaders will be chosen,
but strictly confined to their job of leading—
unless of course they also happen to possess

political insight. The politically intelligent and well informed will make the plans ; but unless they happen to have some talent for personal command or blandishment they will never come out into the open where they might risk making fools of themselves among their fellows. A chief of staff is not expected to waste his time on the parade grounds or in the field ; it is his business to think, to plan campaigns, not to give orders, to encourage the troops or hypnotize them by his personality into a state of courageous enthusiasm. If, like Napoleon or Caesar, he knows how to hypnotize as well as to make plans, let him by all means use his talent, provided that he can spare the time. But if he lacks the gift, he had better delegate the work to somebody who has it ; he, meanwhile, can get on with his job. An army is only a peculiarly and (for all ordinary unmilitary purposes) unnecessarily well-organized state within a state. It may be regarded as a state in a chronic state of crisis ; hence its abnormal and inhuman efficiency. No army which was not inhumanly efficient could hope to win a battle. A state in all respects like an army would be a horrible thing. Nevertheless the military example is not wholly to be neglected. An organization which is moulded by danger and can react efficiently and intelligently to the rudest shocks is not to be despised. If it has been found necessary in armies to separate leadership from planning,

we may feel certain that there is a good practical reason for doing so. The aristocratic
state will have its chief of staff as well as its
officers in personal contact with the men. In
the contemporary democratic state the chief
of staff must also be an officer in the field—an
officer, moreover, who has got to get himself
elected by his men before he can command,
or rather persuade, them to do what he wants.
In the existing circumstances the surprising
fact is, not that there are charlatans in politics,
but that there are any genuine statesmen.

THE ESSENCE OF RELIGION

MERE AND REAL

'Religion,' says Professor Whitehead, 'is what the individual does with his own solitude. . . . If you are never solitary, you are never religious. Collective enthusiasms, revivals, institutions, churches, rituals, Bibles, codes of behaviour, are the trappings of religion, its passing forms. They may be useful or harmful. The end of religion is beyond all this.' Commenting on these words, Dean Inge has remarked that 'they emphasize the difference between the mere practice of religion and its real essence.' 'The *mere* practice of religion and its *real* essence.' It is a phrase that carries immediate conviction to the hasty and incautious reader. '*Mere* practice,' '*real* essence.' The distinction is luminous. Goats are instantaneously divided from sheep. All right-thinking men must be Real Essencers. Bludgeoned by that 'real,' made to feel contemptible by that gratuitous 'mere,' the timid reader throws up his hands and surrenders. True, he enjoys attending service at the Dean's own cathedral : and when he hears an anthem sung by those beautifully pure boy voices, he feels himself becoming all goodness and spirit. But it is a weakness, and if he imagines that he is being religious, he is mistaken. Anthems sung by well-trained choir boys—those are the *mere* practice of religion. The real essence lies elsewhere. Speaking from his evening-paper pulpit, the Dean has said so, and surely a Dean should know.

Poor timid reader! Hasty and incautious believer! A little reflection would reassure the one and make the other withdraw his too easily given assent. Does the Dean know what the real essence of religion is—or of anything else for that matter? If he does, he is to be congratulated; for he knows something which nobody on this earth ever has known or ever will know, until humanity learns to look without human eyes, and to understand with some other instrument than the human mind. Even a Dean of St. Paul's possesses merely human faculties. Real essences are as totally unknowable to him as they are to the rest of us. When he says that solitude is the real essence of religion, what he means is simply this: that solitary religion is the kind of religion which appeals to him, and that he personally can dispense with religious practices. Had he desired to be merely accurate, he would have written otherwise. ' I (together with a certain number of other people, including Professor Whitehead),' it is this that he would have written, ' have a strong bias in favour of purely spiritual, solitary religion divorced from formal practice, and am left cold by ritual, the corybantic emotionalism of revivals, and, in general, by all forms of mechanically organized social religion.'

This would have been the statement of a fact, but a statement quite without the power to move the reader or persuade him into agreement. The natural reaction to such a statement is, ' Indeed ? Very interesting, I 'm sure.' But the Dean, like all the rest of us, desires to move and persuade—desires, indeed, more than the rest of us, probably ; for to persuade is his duty, to move men belongs to his profession. Actuated by this desire to persuade, he declares, quite impersonally, as though he were stating some generally known and obvious truth, that solitude is the real essence of religion. He promotes his personal preference to the status of a natural law. Readers who would simply have shrugged their shoulders if he had said, ' I happen to have a liking for solitariness in my religion,' will listen respectfully to the majestically impersonal generalization : ' Solitariness is the real essence of religion.' The Great Pyramid is more impressive than a sand castle.

DIGRESSION CONCERNING SOPHISMS

It may be noted, in passing, that whenever authors make use of such locutions as ' real essence ' and ' higher truth,' whenever they speak of ideas as being ' natural,' ' inherently right,' ' approved by universal consent,' or by ' all right-thinking men,' they are simply decking out their own strongly held and emotionally tinged convictions or prejudices in disguises which will impress the reader. ' Higher truth ' sounds incomparably better than ' my opinion,' and ' all right-thinking men are agreed ' carries much more conviction than plain ' I think.' The political leader-writer makes a daily use of these simple but perennially effective sophisms. In cases where, if he were merely telling the unvarnished truth, he would write, ' The proprietor of this paper thinks that so and so ought or ought not to be done, and since he thinks so, I am compelled to write as though I too thought so, under penalty of losing my job,' he affirms that ' there is a growing conviction among the electors that so and so ought to be done,' or that ' the country is indignant at the Government's failure to do so and so,' or that ' public opinion is emphatically on the side of so and so.' A moment's reflection is enough to convince any sane person that nobody can possibly know what the majority of electors, or the country, or that mysterious entity ' public opinion,' thinks about any subject. But apparently the necessary moment for reflection is seldom found ; one is forced to the conclusion that most of the readers of newspaper articles are really impressed by all those overwhelming majorities of electors and right-thinking men that figure so prominently in the leaders. If they were not impressed by them, the leader-writers would never trot them out with such monotonous regularity. One of the ways of inducing the majority to accept one's own opinion is to pretend that one's own opinion is that of the majority. And if at the same time one affirms that it is also the opinion of Nature, Pure Reason, and God, then one will have a still better chance of persuading one's fellows. There are, of course, countless other rhetorical tricks besides those which I have mentioned. Mostly unconsciously, but often, too, with complete awareness of what we are doing, we constantly employ them. Ridicule, for example, is one of the commonest and simplest devices for discrediting an opponent. A mild example of its use may be found at the beginning of this essay, where I have treated the Dean with a certain pawky playfulness calculated to make him appear slightly absurd, and so to discredit his opinion in advance. With this exposure of my own little game I shall close a long but not irrelevant parenthesis. The ' essence of religion ' awaits discussion.

VARIETIES OF RELIGIOUS EXPERIENCE

Solitariness with its corollary, informal 'spirituality,' is the essence of religious life. As it

175

happens, I feel in what I imagine to be much the same way as do Dean Inge and Professor Whitehead. Such religious life as I have is purely solitary. The spectacle of people who are never alone or in silence, whose life is one continuous round of social activity, who never stop to meditate or recollect themselves, fills me with all the Dean's uncomprehending amazement. Like him I am little moved by ritual or mass-emotionalism : and when I am so moved, I feel what is perhaps an unreasonable mistrust of the motion. But because I have a bias in favour of solitariness, I do not for that reason affirm that solitariness is the real essence of religion, any more than I maintain that, because my hair is dark brown, the real essence of all hair is to be dark brown. All that I feel justified in saying is that solitary religion is the kind of religion that appeals to me, and apparently also to Dean Inge and Professor Whitehead. In these matters, says Cardinal Newman, ' egotism is true modesty. In religious enquiry each of us can speak only for himself. His own experiences are enough for himself, but he cannot speak for others : he cannot lay down the law ; he can only bring his own experiences to the common stock of psychological facts.' Let the Dean and the Professor speak for themselves ; they are not psychologically qualified to speak for those who find satisfaction only in a social, ' unspiritual ' religion. For these people, it would seem, the letter produces the spirit, the symbol creates the reality symbolized. Without the formal act of devotion they are unable to realize the God to whom the worship is addressed ; the rite brings God into their minds. In a certain sense the rite for them *is* God ; the tangible symbol *is* the spirit. Natural Quakers cannot understand this, and condemn as mere idolaters and formalists the men and women whose minds do not work in the same way as theirs. They might as well blame them for the colour of their eyes or the shape of their noses. In any case it is impossible for them, with their alien mentality, to realize what exactly the formalists do get out of their kind of religion. A man who categorically affirms that solitude is the real essence of religion thereby confesses himself incapable of feeling as the sociable formalists feel. If formalists were to affirm that rites, codes of morals, sacred books, and so forth, constituted the essence of religion, they would be just as much or as little in the right as Dean Inge and Professor Whitehead when the latter dismiss such things as ' mere practice,' and situate the ' real essence ' in solitariness. Like the Dean and the Professor, they would be simply raising their own preferences to the rank of a natural, even a supernatural, law.

SOLITARIES AND SOCIABLES

It is possible that the religion of solitude may be in some sort superior to social and formalized religion. What is certain is that it appeared later in the course of evolution. Furthermore, the founders of the most historically important religions and sects have all, with the exception of Confucius, been solitaries. It would perhaps be true to say that the more powerful and original a mind, the more it will incline towards the religion of solitude, the less it will be drawn towards social religion or be moved by its practices. By its very superiority the religion of solitude is condemned to be the religion of the few. For the great majority of men and women religion still means, what it has always meant, formalized social religion, an affair of rituals, mechanical observances, mass-emotions. Ask any of these people what the real essence of religion is, and they will reply that it consists in the due observation of certain forms, the repetition of certain phrases, the coming together at certain times and in certain places, the working up by appropriate means of communal emotions. And replying thus, they speak the truth, their truth, just as Dean Inge speaks his when he states that the real essence of religion is solitariness. Which of these real essences is the realer one ? Only an extra-mundane judge can answer that question. All that a merely human judge can say is this : the people who find that the real essence of religion is solitariness are on the whole superior (humanly speaking) to those who like their religion social. Whether this means that the solitude - lovers get nearer to the ultimate reality perceived by religious intuition it is difficult to say. In order to answer this we should have first to answer two other questions. Does the religious (and with it the artistic) intuition apprehend an objective reality outside the private psychological universe of the person who feels the intuition ? and is a mind that is superior according to human standards absolutely superior ? Your answer to the first of these questions depends on the intensity of your intuitions. For those in whom they are very strong the reality of the objects they apprehend seems too obvious to be discussed. Those in whom they are weak naturally tend to doubt the existence of something about which they have no information. Assuming that the things which appear to be the object of religious intuition do really exist, we may say that both the solitary and the social worshipper apprehend ultimate reality, each according to his capacities and his peculiar idiosyncrasies. Each has a right to call his own version of reality the only one, in precisely the same way as every man has a right to say that what he finds pleasant is therefore uniquely pleasant. The philosopher perceives that there are as many unique versions as there are apprehending individuals, but that they may be classified according to types. Only an extra-mundane arbitrator can decide which of the two types of version is the truer, which mode of intuition is the more effective as an instrument of knowledge. Our natural human tendencies would be to affirm that the humanly superior mind sees further into reality than the humanly inferior. It may be so, or it may not. But even if it were so, we should not be justified in saying that the religion of the superior individuals was religion in its essence. I do not claim to be anything but all too human, and shall confine myself to making a few remarks on the past and present relations between those for whom the real essence of religion is solitude and pure ' spirituality ' and those for whom it is ' mere practice ' (in the words of Dean Inge) and sociableness.

THE TRANSFORMATION OF SOLITARY INTO SOCIAL RELIGIONS

All the founders of the great historical religions (except Confucius, of whom I shall have more to say later) have been solitaries and spirituals. But the established religions to which they have given their names are all, in the main, social and formal. The story of the way in which the solitary and spiritual Chris-

tianity of Jesus became a social religion of forms
and codes, of rites, traditional gestures, and
pomps, is too familiar to need rehearsing here.
Buddhism passed through the same de-solitariz-
ing and de-spiritualizing process. Gautama
had expounded a metaphysic and a renuncia-
tory way of life : his immediate disciples were
monks and nuns. Buddhism, after the death
of its founder, was an imperfectly organized
religion of asceticism. In the first century of
our era what is called the Mahayana or Great
Vehicle was created, and Buddhism became an
entirely new religion, with a pantheon of Bodhis-
attvas, a noble liturgy, a moving and pompous
ritual. The old Chaitya or meeting-hall of the
Buddhists had already lost much of its primitive simplicity before the formulation of the
Mahayana ; symbolic art had invaded the
Quaker meeting-house. The new Buddhist
temples were now as splendid, as rich in sensuous
appeal, as those of the Hindus. Sculpture,
music, and painting ; the symbolical pageantry
of ritual ; incense, vestments, and banners—
nothing was lacking which might help to produce in the minds of the worshippers that
heavily charged devotional feeling which the
Indians call *bhakti*. At a later date the Tantric
reformation introduced worship of goddesses,
together with a rich collection of magical and
erotic rites. In vain, however, so far as India
was concerned. Hinduism so prodigally gave

the sociable and the unspiritual what they wanted, that it was useless to compete with it. Buddhism might offer deities, ritual, magic, eroticism. Hinduism, with the calm assurance of a J. P. Morgan at a picture sale, just doubled the bid. Buddhism has disappeared out of India; its successes have been in countries where the rival religions have not been so formidably rich as Hinduism in all that buys men's souls.

The history of Islam has been rather different from that of Christianity and Buddhism. It has not suffered such radical changes in the direction of sociableness and unspirituality, for the good reason that it was not, as originally propounded, so solitary or so spiritual as either of the other world religions. Mahomet seems to have been a solitary ; but he was also a practical psychologist. The religion which he offered for the world's acceptance was not a religion of solitude and pure spirituality. Hence its enduring success. The religions of Jesus, of Gautama, of Lao-Tsze have never appealed to more than a few Christians, Buddhists, Taoists. To satisfy the majority of the followers of these teachers new and de-spiritualized social religions have had to be invented. Mahomet's followers have been able to practise without modification the religion which he propounded. The performance of a few simple mechanical acts (such as the repetition of prayers so many times a day), the holding of a few easily comprehended dogmas, are enough to make a man a good Mahometan. Periodic revivalism and the evoking of great mass-emotions on such occasions as pilgrimages provide the necessary emotional excitement and create in the mind of the ordinary Moslem the God whom he is adapted to worship. (It is worth remarking that religions which despise ritual, images, music, and the various pomps which are calculated to produce *bhakti*, are peculiarly liable to outbreaks of revivalism. Revivalism is much commoner in strictly Protestant than in Catholic countries ; for irregular emotional stimuli seem to be required to take the place of those slight but regular recurrent stimuli provided by ritual. The total amount of emotion provided by the different religions may be the same ; but the dosage in which it is given is different. As a believer in order and the decencies, a lover of the arts, I prefer the Catholic method to that of the corybantic Protestants.)

The case of Confucius is unique. Other countries besides China have had traditions of gentlemanly decency. But nowhere except in China has the gentleman's code assumed the proportions of a great religion, nowhere else has the codifier, the original arch-gentleman and scholar, been regarded as a religious leader. Confucius was no solitary, and his mind was so excessively matter-of-fact that he seems not to have preoccupied himself in the least with gods and other worlds, only with man's behaviour in this. It may be doubted whether his doctrines would ever have been widely accepted if he had not incorporated into his system all the rites and gestures, with all the vague ideas in terms of which these rites and gestures were explained, of the Chinese cult of the dead, immemorial even in Confucius's day, five-and-twenty centuries ago. Confucianism is a rationalist's religion, but a rationalist's religion based on the most ancient of human unreasons, the worship of the dead. Chinamen with a taste for more ritual, more pomp, more mass-excitement than Confucianism, even in combination with ancestor worship, can offer, are always able to find what they want in one of China's other religions—in Buddhism, well impregnated with Tantric sorcery, in the magic rites of Taoism.

This brief historical summary is enough to show that, in this world and apart from any question of 'real essence,' the social and unspiritual religions are of enormous importance. All religious history seems to teach one and the same lesson : that the solitary and the purely spiritual constitute a small minority of the whole population of even the most highly developed communities ; that religions whose 'real essence' is solitude and spirituality can never become universal religions and must, if offered as such, undergo radical transforma-

THE ESSENCE OF RELIGION

tion before humanity will accept them. The
history of Protestantism shows how difficult it
is for a religion which aims at being predominantly spiritual to gain general acceptance.
The religions of pure spirituality and solitariness, such as Quakerism, have been confined to
relatively very small numbers of believers. The
other Protestant religions have either decayed
or, if they have held their own, have done so
by making concessions more or less considerable to sociableness and unspirituality. The
most flourishing Protestant sects are those which
encourage revivalistic practices (in this connection a study of certain American sects and
their dervishes is very instructive) and those
which, like the Church of England, have preserved a measure of Catholic ritual. At the
present time it would seem as though the Church
of England were not content with its existing
modicum of ritual. A large and active section
of Anglicans has asked for more, and has now
actually got what it asked for. By elaborating
what Dean Inge describes as 'mere practices'
the Church of England has probably consoli-
dated its position and increased its chances of
future success. In any case, we may feel quite
certain that Anglicanism will not share the
fate of Lutheranism and Calvinism. Too respectable to make a habit of revivalism, too
traditionally Protestant to permit the multiplication and embellishment of 'mere practices,'

these religions have decayed into insignificance. Their adherents have either seceded to Rome or else have lapsed into nominal irreligion, finding satisfaction for their religious feelings in one of those substitutes for organized religion which I have described in another essay. The recent enormous growth of Catholicism in countries hitherto predominantly Protestant, such as America, England, Germany, and Holland, surprises and alarms some observers. I will not affirm that the phenomenon is not alarming ; but that any one possessing the slightest knowledge of human nature should find it surprising is a fact which in its turn surprises me. Catholicism is probably the most realistic of all Western religions. Its practice is based on a profound knowledge of human nature in all its varieties and gradations From the fetish-worshipper to the metaphysician, from the tired business man to the mystic, from the sentimentalist and the sensualist to the intellectual, every type of human being can find in Catholicism the spiritual nourishment which he or she requires. For the sociable, unspiritual man Catholicism is duly sociable and unspiritual. For the solitary and the spiritual it provides a hermitage and the most exquisite, the profoundest models of religious meditation ; it gives the silence of monasteries and the bareness of the Carthusian church, it offers the devotional introspection of À Kempis and St. Theresa, the subtleties of Pascal and Newman, the poetry of Crashaw and St. John of the Cross and a hundred others. The only people for whom it does not cater are those possessed by that rare, dangerous, and uneasy passion, the passion for liberty.

DEVELOPMENT OF THE RELIGIOUS FACULTIES

Solitary and purely spiritual religion is a later product than social religion, a growth, it would seem, of the last three thousand years. This period is extremely small compared with the stretch of time during which human beings have been human. It is difficult to believe that the faculties of the mind can have changed greatly in a hundred generations. All that we know of the development of life would lead us to believe that the faculties which the solitary uses existed, but in a latent and as yet potential state, long before they were first consciously and successfully employed to explore the ultimate reality of religion. Analogously, we are forced to believe that the mathematical and the musical faculties existed potentially long before they were effectively realized. Musical harmony is the product of the last five hundred years. But who would venture to affirm that a new faculty was almost suddenly introduced in the human mind between fourteen and fifteen hundred Anno Domini? The actualization of hitherto potential faculties is probably more or less similar in all cases. Extraordinarily gifted individuals make the first step ; a threshold is crossed and they become conscious of their powers, and of the entities with which their newly discovered powers enable them to deal. Their action can be imitated. A step which some one has once consciously taken can easily be repeated. Little by little a technique for the exploitation of the newly discovered faculties is elaborated. Using this technique, other extraordinarily gifted individuals are able to explore those aspects of the universe of which the newly developed faculties have made men aware—to explore them with a thoroughness and to an extent which would have seemed inconceivable to their equally gifted predecessors. It is only after the technique of exploiting the faculties has been developed to a certain point that men of genius can be compared. Pythagoras may have been as great a geometrician as Riemann ; but the technique of mathematics had been so little developed in his day that he had to spend his genius struggling with difficulties that for us have ceased to exist. We can compare him with men of his own age, but not with men of ours. It is the same with the Greek musicians ; there may have been composers as remarkable as Beethoven, but their technique of expressing themselves in music was so rudimentary that they are simply not commensurable with Beethoven. Musicians of to-day are commensurable with Beethoven. A comparison between him and our contemporaries is possible ; our contemporaries come out very badly from the test. The whole history of art brings evidence to prove that once the technique of exploiting the faculties has reached a certain pitch, exceptionally gifted individuals can rise to achievements which may remain almost indefinitely unequalled. Thus the technique of exploiting the visual-artistic faculty was very early brought to a high pitch of perfection. Palaeolithic man made pictures of animals which have, quite literally, never been surpassed.

The development of religion is very similar to that of the arts. The faculties employed in solitary communion with ultimate reality were discovered and developed fairly late in man's history (though much earlier than either the musical or mathematical faculties). The technique of exploiting these faculties reached a certain pitch of development, and exceptionally gifted individuals appeared whose achievements in what may be called the art of solitary religion have never been surpassed. It may well be that while man remains biologically man the achievements in their various spheres of Lao-Tsze and Jesus, of Phidias, of Shakespeare, of Beethoven, will remain maximum achievements. What will happen when, and if, humanity develops into something more than human we cannot say. The question is hardly worth thinking about. What is of interest to us is the fact that human faculties do not seem to have been improved or radically changed during the last few thousand years—only more or less effectually developed. Unless something very surprising happens (and a new biological invention may upset all our calculations) there is every reason to suppose that the same state of affairs will hold good for the next few thousand years. Where religion is concerned, this means that the ratio of solitaries to sociables will remain much as it is at present and has been for the past centuries. It means, that is to say, that there will be a few people for whom ' the essence of religion ' is solitude, and a great many for whom it is sociability and ' mere practice.' That all human beings should become spirituals and solitaries is perhaps a desirable consummation (though even this is not entirely certain); but it is something which, quite obviously, is not going to happen for a very long time. For any future near enough to be of interest to ourselves the religious situation will be what it always has been.

If the Dean imagines that by talking about ' real essences ' he is going permanently to transform a single born sociable into a spiritual solitary, he is very much mistaken. The attempt has been made before ; but in spite of all the preachings of all the founders of solitary religions the numerical ratio between the contrasted types has remained, apart from momentary fluctuations, constant. Where Buddha and Jesus have failed, will the Dean of St. Paul's and the Professor of Philosophy at the University of Harvard succeed? I have my doubts.

A NOTE ON DOGMA

DOGMA AND SCIENCE

'The dogmas of religion,' says Professor Whitehead, 'are the attempts to formulate in precise terms the truths disclosed in the religious experience of mankind. In exactly the same way the dogmas of physical science are the attempts to formulate in precise terms the truths disclosed in the sense-perception of mankind.'

The religious experience of mankind is in the nature of a direct apprehension of a 'rightness in things.' Professor Whitehead is not content to take this intuitive experience as he finds it, in the raw. He wants it to be rationalized. 'Reason,' he says, 'is the safeguard of the objectivity of religion; it secures for it the general coherence denied to hysteria.' And again: 'another objection against this appeal to such an intuition, merely experienced in exceptional moments, is that thereby the intuition is a function of these moments.' The rationalization of the intuition guarantees it—in some way which Professor Whitehead never clearly explains—against being a function of the moments in which it is experienced.

Let us briefly examine his claims. Religious dogmas are exactly on the same footing as scientific dogmas ; and reason is the safeguard of the objectivity of religion. The statements are clear —so clear that their falsity is immediately manifest. ' Reason is the safeguard of the objectivity of religion.' Why ? It is certainly not the safeguard of the objectivity of science. The safeguard of the objectivity of science is sense-perception. Scientific theories which are not functions of sense-perceptions are generally nonsensical. The theories in Hegel's Philosophy of Nature are classical examples of scientific theories that are not functions of sense-perception. They are also excessively reasonable, the product of a ratiocination uncontrolled by observation. Does Hegel's reason provide a ' safeguard for the objectivity ' of his theories ? It certainly does not. In their preposterousness they completely justify those famous lines in the Earl of Rochester's *Satire against Man* :

> Reason, an *Ignis Fatuus* of the mind,
> Which leaves the Light of Nature, Sense, behind,
> Pathless and dangerous, wand'ring ways it takes,
> Through Error's fenny bogs and thorny Brakes,
> While the misguided Follower climbs with pain
> Mountains of Whimseys heapt in his own brain.

When these words were written, Hegel's philosophy was something hidden in the distant future. Unconsciously a prophet, Rochester was referring to an only too familiar past. The scientific theories of the Schoolman were as reasonable, as pure of all vulgarly empirical observation, and as absurd as those of Hegel. Living in the high heroic dawn of the age of science, Rochester had a natural mistrust of that *ignis fatuus* which had led St. Thomas and his followers through such dark and circuitous ways back to the profound ignorance of external nature from which they started.

If, as Professor Whitehead affirms, the dogmas of religion are precisely like those of science, then we must believe that what is true of scientific dogmas is also true of the dogmas of religion, and that reason, uncontrolled by observation, is no guarantee of the objectivity of such dogmas. The man of science is perfectly ready to admit that his theory is a function of the moments of sense-perception. He does not mind admitting this, because that which is perceived at these moments is for all practical purposes the same, not only for himself at different periods, but for all other observers. The theologian objects to admitting that his theory is a function of his moments of religious intuition, for the good reason that his intuitions are different at different moments and that the intuitions of all men are by no means identical. For, while we may admit that the sense of values—the sense that one thing, one course of action is better, and another worse—is universal, we cannot truthfully affirm that the more general intuition of a 'rightness in things,' in the world at large, is universal or even chronic in one individual. On a bright spring day, when I am feeling particularly well, when I am happily in love and my affairs are successful, I may have a direct intuition of the rightness of things. But in the winter, afflicted, as I feel, unjustly by the inclemencies of fate, frustrated in my ambitions, rejected by my lovers, I may equally well feel a direct intuition of the complete ethical indifference of the universe. Why should the rationalization of the one mood be more objective than the rationalization (which may be equally logical) of the other? What reason have we for supposing that Browning's optimistic 'God's in His Heaven, all's right with the world,' is superior as objective truth to Hardy's assertion that the heaven is empty, or, if tenanted, entirely careless of the world? The answer is, that we have no reason, only our intuition. Each person will choose the rationalization which suits his prevailing or his passing mood. All that for each individual is absolutely certain is that at a given moment he has a certain intuition about things in general. He may, if he chooses, rationalize his intuition and assert, as Professor Whitehead does, that this rationalization guarantees the objective truth of his intuition. But all that it does in fact guarantee is that his intuition is of a certain kind, and that it lends itself to a certain kind of rationalization. It offers no guarantee against other men and women experiencing intuitions of a different kind and rationalizing them in quite a different way.

VARIETY OF HUMAN TYPES

The dissimilarities between human beings are as radical as their resemblances. Their physiological structure and perhaps, as Jung plausibly suggests, the unconscious foundations of their psychological structure are very similar in all. Except when they suffer from obvious bodily disabilities, the effects of which can easily be discounted, men see, hear, feel, taste, smell in very much the same sort of way. They are ' fed with the same food, hurt with the same weapons, subject to the same diseases, healed by the same means, warmed and cooled by the same winter and summer.' And, according to Jung, they are haunted in the depths of their unconsciousness by the same primordial images. It is in the way they make use of these similar sensations that they differ. ' Some men there are,' to quote Shylock once more,

> Some men there are love not a gaping pig ;
> Some, that are mad if they behold a cat ;
> And others, when the bagpipe sings i' the nose,
> Cannot contain their urine.

The sight of pig and cat, the sound of bagpipes are the same, regarded abstractly as pure sensations, for all men. But to these, for all practical purposes, identical sensations individuals react in the most unexpectedly diverse ways. In the abstract, instincts and emotions, reason, intuition, the special abilities and so forth, may be regarded as the same, or at any rate similar, in all men. The fact that these mental functions can be named and abstracted by the classifying mind is in itself a proof of their qualitative similarity. But in the living individual they are combined in such an endless variety of ways, in such a diversity of proportions, that one personality regarded as a whole is irreducibly different from another. Water is extremely unlike peroxide of hydrogen ; yet both are composed of the same elements. Their dissimilarity is due to the fact that the elements are combined in different proportions. The elements — hereditary and environmental — of which a human personality is composed are without number, and can be combined in dosages ranging from the infinitesimally small, or even the non-existent, to the enormous. The surprising thing is not that men should be so unlike, but that they should be as similar as they are. The chemical analogy would lead one to expect an even greater divergency between man and man than that which we actually find. The addition of an extra atom of oxygen to a molecule of water is sufficient to transmute the stuff we drink into the stuff that turns

brown barmaids into blondes and kills bacilli.
A man with an extra talent or two, an abnormally large dose of intelligence, fantasy, and
intuition, is probably a very remarkable man ;
but he is still quite recognizably a man. Oxy-
genated water, on the other hand, is no longer
water. Perhaps we should regret that human
beings do not behave like chemicals. The
reason presumably why they do not is that they
have at all costs to survive. The biological
pressure under which men live is enormous ;
it sets a limit to the possible variations of mind
as well as body. Where chemical elements
find themselves in conditions analogous to
those in which human beings pass their existence, they too can only combine to a very
limited extent. At the centre of the earth
there is much less chemical variety than at the
surface. If men were to live where there is
no biological pressure, they would doubtless
exhibit all the diversity of chemicals on the
earth's surface. But even as things actually
are, the differences between man and man
are still considerable—how considerable I have
shown in another essay. The faculty which
we call religious intuition resembles reason,
memory, and emotion in so far as it is a
variable quantity. All men have similar sensations, but not all have similar intuitions. Religious intuitions differ in intensity, not only as
between man and man, but in the same man

at different moments. Given light and normal
eyes, all of us on all occasions see very much
the same things—which does not mean, of
course, that we make the same use of what we
see, or that these more or less identical sensations carry an identical meaning for each
beholder. But the religious intuition is not the
same on all occasions. The mystic's ecstasy,
for example, is of rare occurrence. Plotinus
could see the sky every day, and as often in each
day as he chose to raise his eyes. But it is recorded of him that he saw God only three times in
his life. The majority of human beings never see
God—at any rate in the way in which Plotinus
or Boehme saw God. If they have religious
intuitions—and some of them seem to go through
life without having any first-hand knowledge of
the religious experience — these intuitions are
quite unlike those of the mystics, not merely in
intensity, but also in kind. The nature of the
rationalization is strictly determined by the
nature of the intuition. Thus the typical mystic
has the sensation of being absorbed into God.
In her autobiography St. Theresa has described
the stages in her ' ascent towards God.' Deliberate meditation on a religious theme is followed
by ' the orizon of quiet ' ; this, in its turn, is
succeeded by ' the sleep of the powers,' which
leads on, in the final ecstasy or flight of the
spirit into God, to something very like loss
of consciousness. The spirit is annihilated as

an individual entity, it ceases in the ultimate somnambulistic state of rapture to exist. It is perfectly possible, however, to have a religious experience without losing consciousness ; to be vividly aware of God without for an instant ceasing to be aware of oneself as an individual. It is obvious that these two types of religious experience will quite naturally tend to be rationalized in different ways. The man who preserves his own identity while being aware of God will tend to envisage the universe as something real existing separately from its creator. The mystic who feels himself in the moment of ecstasy becoming something absolutely different from his ordinary self will tend as naturally to rationalize his experience in terms of some other philosophy ; he will explain his experience by saying that the world in itself is only an appearance, that it is real only in so far as it partakes of God's reality, which is the only thing that exists. Thus we see that the two contrasted philosophies of transcendence and pantheism are the rationalization of two different intuitions. Which of these two dogmas is true ? It is impossible to say, because there is no impartial person to judge. One is true to the man who has one kind of religious experience, the other is true to the man whose intuition of God is of another kind. No universally valid scientific theories would be possible in a society where some individuals were smaller than ants, and had eyes that could see filter-passing microbes ; where others were ordinary human beings, and yet others disembodied spirits capable of travelling with the velocity of light and having no sense of temporal duration. What would be true for individuals of one type would seem entirely meaningless to those of another. Our existing scientific theories may not be absolutely true—in fact they quite certainly are not. But they do mean roughly the same to all human beings, because all human beings have roughly the same sensations. Any one who has normal sense organs and who knows the rules of the logical game can test, not the absolute, but the relative, temporary human truth of any scientific theory. With theological dogmas it is different. Not only are they not absolutely true—it is impossible for any human theory to be that. They do not mean the same to all human beings. Where the perceptions are different, the rationalizations of those perceptions are incommensurable. The people who perceive God as something transcending a real and definite universe cannot in the nature of things understand the theology of men who perceive God as the sole all-embracing reality—a reality which at ordinary times we very imperfectly grasp, but into which on occasions it is possible for us to melt and be absorbed. Religious writers constantly complain that those who disagree with them are blind as bats and deaf as adders. And so they are. To the vision they see, to the heavenly music they hear, their opponents are indeed blind and deaf. They themselves are no less blind and deaf in relation to what their opponents see and hear. Each side blames the other, and each believes itself to be exclusively in the right. And from the pragmatic standpoint this is entirely as it should be. Those who believe that they are exclusively in the right are generally those who achieve something. The heroes of action are rarely sceptical philosophers. If Sancho had been a Crusader or an Inquisitor, he would not have suffered Don Quixote to tell him that he was talking nonsense. He would have knocked him down, or at least bludgeoned him with arguments. Being only a sceptical philosopher, 'Why, truly, sir,' quoth Sancho, 'if you do not understand me, no wonder if my sentences be thought nonsense. But let that pass, I understand myself.'

PARADOX

Is Sancho's the last word on the matter? It is the last a sceptic can utter. But the Church has uttered a still later one. It has spoken in paradoxes. It has said that God is both many and one, both transcendent and immanent ; that He has foreknowledge, but that man none the less has free will ; that He

is perfectly good, but that He nevertheless
foresaw the fall, and, foreseeing, was to that
extent responsible for all the evil and pain of
the world. *Credo quia absurdum est.* Tertullian, it
seems, never used those words ; but he ought to
have used them, and since he did not, men have
found it necessary to invent them. For any
theory which is to cover all the human facts
must necessarily be absurd, since the facts contradict one another and yet co-exist. The intuitions which different human beings have
had about the nature of God are irreconcilably
different. Some men have perceived God as a
personal being, others as an impersonal being,
others again have perceived that He does not
exist. Some have perceived Him as existing
apart from the world, others as containing the
world and forming its substance, others have
perceived that the world itself is God. Some
have had an intuition of an enemy, others of
a friend ; some have felt God as angry, others
as loving. Some have known that God approved
of abstinence, others that He is well pleased
with Dionysiac revelry. Some have seen Him
symbolized as a Phallus, others as an instrument of torture. There are scores of other
ways in which men have perceived their God,
and every intuition has been more or less
logically and systematically rationalized. No
conception of the nature of God can be true
—humanly true, I mean ; for we can leave

absolute truth out of account as unattainable
—which does not cover all the facts of human
experience. And since, in this matter, as in so
many others, human experience is multifarious
and self-contradictory, no conception of the
nature of God is true which is not also multifarious and self-contradictory. My only objection to Catholic theology is, not that it is absurd,
but that it is not absurd enough. It is realistic
up to a point—much more realistic than many
of the self-styled modern and scientific philosophies which have risen in its place—but it
has not dared to be realistic to the end. The
truth is paradoxical ; but man's passion for
rational coherence is even stronger than his
love of truth. The theologians have perceived
that the feelings and spiritual perceptions of
men are irreducibly different among themselves. They have rationalized some of these
different intuitions in the form of paradoxical
dogmas. But they have shrunk from rationalizing all the intuitions, from making their doctrines not merely absurd, but extravagantly
absurd. They were driven prematurely into
unparadoxical consistency by their belief that
one of the intuitions to be rationalized was
not a human intuition, but a perception by
a divine being of absolute truth. The remarkable thing is, that having this belief, the theologians went as far along the road of paradox
as they did. Those who do not share their

belief find it unnecessary to stop where they stopped or impose any arbitrary limit to the number of irreducible intuitions admissible for rationalization.

That the ultimate reality is unknowable is no reason why we should not speculate about its nature. Our intuitions of its character are varied and contradictory. But we need not, for that reason, suppose that the reality itself is anything but single and consistent. The paradox is not in it ; it is in us. We create the difficulties which perplex our minds. The devils who in Milton's hell discussed ' fixed fate, free will, foreknowledge absolute,' were probably racking their brains over a bogus problem of their own (considering that they were devils) all too human manufacture. But though in itself the ultimate reality may not be self-contradictory, it remains for us, in our present state of consciousness, a paradox. It is perceived as one thing by one man, as some-thing entirely different by another ; it is even perceived as different things at different moments by the same individual. We know of no im-partial judge to decide which is the true per-ception. Arbitrarily to select one intuition as correct is not to solve the problem. It is merely to shirk it. Facts do not cease to exist because they are ignored. For the practical purposes of worship each man must obviously accept his own intuition as the best. It may be a poor thing, but it is his own and all he possesses. The philosopher cannot imitate the practical man. A religious theory, if it is to be universally valid, must cover all the facts. It must, in Professor Whitehead's words, ' formulate in precise terms the truths disclosed in the religious experience of mankind.' The religious experience of mankind is diverse to the point of self-contradiction. It follows that the theory in which the truths disclosed by this experience are formulated must be paradoxical and absurd. The beautifully rational simplicity of Professor Whitehead's theology is the chief argument against its validity. Nothing so simple and so rational can possibly be true.

THE SUBSTITUTES FOR RELIGION

THE UNCHANGING FOUNDATIONS

The horses and bisons on the walls of the palaeolithic cave-man's dwelling might have been painted by an artist of the twentieth century—that is, if there were any contemporary artists with sufficient talent to paint them. The earliest surviving literatures are still entirely comprehensible. And though the earliest philosophies and religions may seem intellectually very remote from ourselves, we feel, none the less, that the emotions and intuitions to which they give rational, or pseudo-rational, expression are recognizably akin to our own. Rationalizations change, and with them the rules of conduct based upon rationalizations. But what is rationalized does not change. At most a latent power is developed; the potential is made actual; a technique is discovered for realizing and exploiting faculties hitherto useless and unrealized. In their likenesses and unlikenesses the men of to-day resemble the men of the past. There were introverts and extroverts in the time of Homer, intellectuals and intuitives, visualizers and non-visualizers, just as there are now. And in all probability the relative numbers of individuals belonging to the various types have remained more or less constant throughout history. Neither the hereditary differences between men, nor the similarities, have greatly varied. What has varied has been the vehicles of thought and action by means of which the hereditarily constant differences and similarities have been expressed. The form of institutions and philosophies may change ; but the substance that underlies them remains indestructible, because the nature of humanity remains unaltered.

THE DECAY OF RELIGION

The case of religion might seem, at a first glance, to disprove this statement. During the last two or three hundred years the religions of the West have manifestly decayed. There have been ups, it is true, as well as downs ; but the downward movement has predominated, with the result that we are living to-day in what is probably the most irreligious epoch of all history. And yet religion is the rationalization of feelings and intuitions which we have just assumed to be substantially unchangeable. Is the assumption wrong, and has our nature radically altered during the past few generations ? Alternatively, must we believe that religion is not the rationalization of deep-seated feelings and intuitions, but a mere fantastical whimsy, invented and re-invented by every generation for its own amusement ? The dilemma is apparent, not real. The fact that religions have decayed during the past few generations does not mean that they are definitively dead. And the fact that many people are now without a religion does not mean that they are without some substitute for a religion ; their religious feelings and intuitions may be rationalized in forms not immediately recognizable as religious.

That whole classes of mental functions and faculties may fall into temporary disrepute is abundantly evidenced by history, which makes it no less clear that the attempt to suppress a part of the being, to live without it, as though it did not exist, is never permanently successful. Sooner or later the outlawed elements take their revenge, the order of their banishment is rescinded, and a new philosophy of life becomes popular—a philosophy which gives to previously despised and outlawed elements their due place in the scheme of things, and often, in the heat of reaction, more than their due place. There is no reason to believe that the present condition of irreligion is a permanent one. The partially educated masses, it is true, have just discovered, some forty years behind the time, the materialism of nineteenth-century science. But the scientific men, it is significant to note, are rapidly abandoning the materialistic position. What they think now, the masses will doubtless be thinking a generation hence.

The decay of religion is not only in all probability temporary ; it is also incomplete. The religious instincts of those who have no recognized religion (I leave out of account the still considerable and growing numbers of those who have) find expression in a surprising variety of non-religious ways. Lacking religion, they have provided themselves with substitutes for it. It is of these surrogates that I now propose to write.

NATURE OF THE GENUINE ARTICLE

The surrogates of a thing cannot be intelligently discussed unless something is known about the nature of the genuine article. Only some one who has tasted butter can criticize the different brands of margarine. It is the same with the substitutes for religion. Unless we start with some preliminary idea of the nature of religion, we shall be unable to recognize, much less evaluate, its substitutes.

I shall not attempt to give a formal definition of religion. Such definitions are mostly so vague and abstract as to be almost meaningless. What is required for our purposes is not a definition of religion so much as a catalogue of the principal states of mind and actions recognized as religious, together with a brief account of the most characteristic features of the religious doctrines which are the rationalizations of these states and acts.

THE SUBSTITUTES FOR RELIGION

A sense of awe in face of the mysteries and immensities of the world—this, I suppose, is the most fundamental religious state of mind. This feeling is rationalized in the form of belief in supernatural beings, both kindly and malevolent, as is the world in which men live. In the higher religions the rationalization is very elaborate and constitutes an account, complete and coherent, of the whole universe.

The religious feeling finds its active as opposed to its intellectual expression in the form of propitiatory ritual. Ritual, as soon as it is invented, occupies a place of prime importance in all religions. For the rite evokes by association those emotions of awe which are, for the individual who feels them, the god himself. And these emotions are accompanied by others no less exhilarating, and therefore no less divine. Chief among these is what may be called the social emotion, the feeling of excitement caused by being in a crowd.

Asceticism is common to all religions. It is unnecessary to try to explain why men should have believed that they could win the favours of the gods by abstaining from pleasure and comfort. The fact that they have done so is enough for us.

Human misery is so great and so widespread that one of the principal functions of religion has been that of consolation, and one of the most typical religious doctrines is that of future compensatory states.

211

Absoluteness is a quality typical of religious beliefs. Religious doctrines are held with a passionate tenacity. If what is believed is absolutely true, then it is of vital importance that the believer should cling to his belief and refuse to admit the contrary beliefs of others. Conversely, absoluteness of belief, resulting from whatever cause, tends to create a certainty of the absolute reality of the thing believed in. The quality of the faith is transferred to its object, which thereby becomes absolute and consequently worthy of worship.

All religions have priests, who fulfil a double function. They are, in the first place, to use M. Paul Valéry's expressive phrase, *les préposés aux choses vagues*—mediators between man and the surrounding mystery, which they understand and can propitiate more effectually than ordinary folk. Their second function is earthly ; they are confessors, advisers, casuists, spiritual doctors ; at certain periods they have also been rulers.

Such are a few of the most obviously significant facts about religion. With these in mind, we may proceed to consider its substitutes. The first thing that strikes us is, that none of the substitutes is more than very partially adequate. A religion covers all the intellectual and emotional ground. It offers an explanation of the universe, it consoles, it provides its devotees with uplifting, god-creating rites. No substitute can do as much ; one offers rites, but not philosophy ; another compensatory doctrines, but no rites. And so on. No religious surrogate can completely satisfy all the religious needs of men. Much of the restlessness and uncertainty so characteristic of our time is probably due to the chronic sense of unappeased desires from which men naturally religious, but condemned by circumstances to have no religion, are bound to suffer.

THE POLITICAL SURROGATE

Perhaps the most important substitute for religion is politics. Extreme nationalism presents its devotees with a god to be worshipped —the Country—together with much inspiring ritual of a mainly military kind. In most countries and for most of their inhabitants nationalism is a spasmodic faith, of which the believers are only occasionally conscious. But where the state is weak and in danger, where men are oppressed by a foreign ruler, it becomes an unflagging enthusiasm. Even in countries where there is no sense of inferiority to be compensated, where there are no immediate dangers and no oppressors, the nationalist substitute for religion is often continuously inspiring. I have met some few admirable men and women for whom, unlike Nurse Cavell, patriotism was quite enough. The country was to be served and worshipped. They asked, as far as I could discover, for no other god. The only universe of which they demanded an explanation was the universe of politics. And with what a simple, unpretentious explanation even of that they were contented !

Extreme democracy has as many devotees as extreme nationalism ; and among those devotees there are probably more chronic enthusiasts than are to be found among the patriots. As a substitute for religion, extreme democracy is more adequate than nationalism ; for it covers more ground, at any rate as a doctrine. For revolutionary democracy is a forward-looking faith. It preaches a future state—in this world, not another—when all the injustices of the present will be remedied, all the unhappinesses compensated, when the first shall be last and the last first, and there shall be crowns for all and no more weeping, and practically no more work. Moreover, it is susceptible of a much more thorough philosophical treatment than nationalism. ' My country right or wrong ' is a sentiment which cannot be completely rationalized. The only reason that any man has for loving and serving his country is the mere accident that it happens to be his. He knows that if he had been born somewhere else the object of his worship would have been different. Not the bulldog, but the cock or the eagle would have been his totem. Not Dr. Arne, but

Haydn or Rouget de Lisle, would have hymned him into ecstasy. There can be no metaphysic of patriotism ; it is just a raw, unalterable fact, which must be accepted as it is. Democracy, on the other hand, does not vary from country to country ; it is a universal and imperishable doctrine—for the poor are everywhere and at all times with us. The raw facts of misery, envy, and discontent can be rationalized in the most thorough-going fashion. To explain and justify the very natural desire of the poor and oppressed for freedom, wealth, and power a far-reaching system of metaphysics has been evolved. The Christian doctrines of original sin and divine grace have been denied, and all the virtues and perfections of God have been lodged in humanity—not indeed as it is now (that would be too hard to swallow), but as it will be when freed from oppression and enlightened by education. This doctrine, although manifestly false, is a genuine religious explanation of the world, in terms of which it is possible, with a little judicious manipulation, to explain all the facts of human life.

Doctrinally, then, revolutionary democracy is an excellent substitute for religion. When it comes to practice, however, it is less satisfying than nationalism. For nationalism has a traditional and highly elaborate ritual of its own. Revolutionary democracy can offer nothing to compare with the royal processions, the military parades, the music pregnant with associations, the flags, the innumerable emblems, by means of which patriotic sentiment can be worked up and the real presence of the mother-land made manifest to every beholder.

The craving for ritual and ceremony is strong and widespread. How strong and how widely spread is shown by the eagerness with which men and women who have no religion, or a puritanical religion without ritual, will seize at any oppor-tunity to participate in ceremonies of whatever kind. The Ku-Klux-Klan would never have achieved its post-war success if it had stuck to plain clothes and committee meetings. Messrs. Simmons and Clark, the resuscitators of that remarkable body, understood their public. They insisted on strange nocturnal ceremonies at which fancy-dress should not be optional but compulsory. Membership went up by leaps and bounds. The Klan had an object : its ritual was symbolical of something. But to a rite - starved multitude, significance is appa-rently superfluous. The popularity of com-munity singing has shown that the rite, as such, is what the public wants. So long as it is impressive and arouses an emotion, the rite is good in itself. It does not much matter what it signifies. The ceremony of community singing lacks all philosophical significance, it has no connection with any system of ideas. It is simply itself and nothing more. The traditional rituals of religion and daily life have largely vanished out of the world. But their disappearance has caused regret. Whenever people have a chance they try to satisfy their hunger for ceremonial, even though the rite with which they appease it be entirely meaningless.

THE ARTISTIC SUBSTITUTE

Art occupies a position of great importance in the modern world. By this I do not mean to imply that modern art is better than the art of other generations. It is obviously not. The quantity, not the quality, of modern art is important. More people take a conscious interest in art as art. And more devote themselves to its practice than at any other period. Our age, though it has produced few masterpieces, is a thoroughly aesthetic age. This increase in the numbers of the practitioners and dilettanti in all the arts is not unconnected with the decrease in the numbers of religious believers. To minds whose religious needs have been denied their normal fulfilment, art brings a certain spiritual satisfaction. In its lowest forms art is like that emotionally charged ritual for ritual's sake so popular, as we have seen, at the present time. In its higher and more significant forms it is philosophy as well as ritual.

The arts, including music and certain important kinds of literature, have been, at most periods, the handmaids of religion. Their principal function was to provide religion with the visible or audible symbols which create in the mind of the beholder those feelings which for him personally are the god. Divorced from religion, the arts are now independently cultivated for their own sake. That aesthetic beauty which was once devoted to the service of God has now set up as a god on its own. The cultivation of art for its own sake has become a substitute for religion. That it is an extremely inadequate substitute must be apparent to any one who has observed the habits of those who lead the pure, aesthetic life. Where beauty is worshipped for beauty's sake as a goddess, independent of and superior to morality and philosophy, the most horrible putrefaction is apt to set in. The lives of the aesthetes are the far from edifying commentary on the religion of beauty.

THE RELIGION OF SEX

Other instances might be given of activities which were once part of religion being isolated and endowed with the significance rightly belonging to the whole. Substitutes for religion which were originally no more than a part of the genuine article are peculiarly unsatisfactory and lead their devotees into impossible situations. A good example of such a partial substitute is the puritanical religion of sexual taboos. Asceticism, as we have seen, is a feature common to most religions, and one which in Christianity has been particularly marked. But it has never been the whole of any religion. Among contemporary 'smuthounds' (to borrow one of Mr. Mencken's expressive coinages) one finds people for whom the cult of sexual purity is in itself a complete substitute for religion. The Christian ascetic restrained all his appetites, greed and covetousness as well as lasciviousness, and he restrained them because he believed that by doing so he was pleasing his God. The modern purity-leaguer has no qualms about money-grubbing and gormandizing : his sole preoccupation is sexual licence, particularly in other people. He is often a free-thinker, so that his campaigns against indecency propitiate no God, but are conducted because they are good in themselves. But are they ? ' *Apud gentiles*,' says St. Thomas, ' *fornicatio simplex non reputabatur illicita propter corruptionem naturalis rationis : Judaei, autem ex lege divina instructi, eam illicitam reputabant*.' It is only on this one point that the free-thinking smuthound accepts divine law. In all other matters he trusts to the corruption of his natural reason. He should be more logical and consistent.

It is a remarkable fact that, while one may say, to all intents and purposes, whatever one likes about religion and politics, while one may publicly preach atheism and communism, one may not make public mention, except in a scientific work, of the most rudimentary physiological facts. In most modern countries the only state-supported orthodoxy is a sexual orthodoxy. There is a powerful religion, or rather pseudo-religion, of sexual purity. It cannot, it is true, boast of many sincerely ardent devotees. But most of the few who genuinely believe in it are fanatics. Defined in psychological terms, a fanatic is a man who consciously overcompensates a secret doubt. The fanatics of puritanism are generally found to be overcompensating a secret prurience. Their influence in the modern world is great out of all proportion to their numbers ; for few people dare, by opposing them, to run the risk of being called immoral, corrupters of youth, dissolvers of the family, and all the rest (the truly virtuous have an inexhaustible armoury of abuse on which to draw. If the smuthounds had a genuine religion to satisfy them, they would probably be less of a nuisance than they are at present. Ages of faith, if one may judge from mediaeval literature, were not ages of puritanism.

BUSINESS

The modern apostles of commerce are trying to persuade people to accept business as a substitute for religion. Money-making, they assert, is a spiritual act ; efficiency and common honesty are a service to humanity. Business in general is the supreme God, and the individual Firm is the subsidiary deity to whom devotions are directly paid. For the ambitious, the boomingly prosperous, and those too much involved in strenuous living to be able to do any strenuous thinking, the worship of business may perhaps supply the lack of genuine religion. But its inadequacy is profound and radical. It offers no coherent explanation of any universe outside of that whose centre is the stock exchange ; in times of trouble it cannot console ; it compensates no miseries ; its ideals are too quickly realizable—they open the door to cynicism and indifference. Its virtues are so easily practised that literally any human being who believes in the religion of Business can imagine himself a truly good man. Hence the appalling self-satisfaction and conscious pharisaism so characteristic of the devotees of business. It is a justificatory religion for the rich and those who would become rich. And even with them it works only when times are good and they are without personal unhappiness. At the first note of a tragedy it loses all its efficacy; the briefest slump is sufficient to make it evaporate. The preachers of this commercial substitute for religion are numerous, noisy, and pretentious. But they can never, in the nature of things, be more than momentarily and superficially successful. Men require a more substantial spiritual nourishment than these are able to provide.

CRANKS

Some human beings are so constituted that almost any idea can take on the qualities of a religious dogma. A condition of absolute belief is reached; the object of belief is itself endowed with absoluteness and so becomes divine; to act on the belief, to serve its deified object, to propagate the truth and combat false doctrine become religious duties. We are all familiar with cranks and the riders of hobbies. Their eccentricities, their absurd and barbarous one-sidedness, are due to the fact that they treat as though it were a religion an idea which has nothing in common with a religious dogma except its quality (for them) of absoluteness. The process by which an idea takes on this religious quality of absoluteness is not the same in all cases. In some cases the absoluteness of a belief is proportionate to the length of time it has been believed. Beliefs received in extreme youth tend to become an integral part

of the mind. To deny a very familiar belief
—one that has become, so to speak, encrusted
with personal associations and tangled in the
feelings—is in a real sense to deny the man
who holds it. But it is not exclusively by the
prescriptive right of mere length of tenure that
ideas become absolute. The crank may acquire
his hobby comparatively late in life. Moreover, it often happens that cranks will ride
several hobbies in succession, treating each in
turn as an absolute and religious dogma. There
is a recognizable crank-mind with a specific
tendency to receive beliefs and endow them
with qualities of absoluteness. How and why
cranks should transform opinions into religions
is somewhat obscure. Cranks, if we may believe
Jung, are extreme extraverts—people whose
whole spiritual tendency is outwards, towards
the object. The object on which their attention fixes itself is an already existing idea, which
they embrace with a love and a faith so exclusive that they are driven to a conscious denial
of everything else, including even their own
self. The self, however, is a living organism,
and refuses to be denied without a struggle.
Conscious devotion to the external idea is
balanced by an unconscious development of
the self-regarding tendencies (for the mind, like
the body, preserves its equilibrium only because
its parts live in a perpetual state of 'hostile
symbiosis'). The crank begins to sacrifice

himself to his idea for personal motives. The outlawed elements of the personality have revenged themselves upon the idea ; but in revenging themselves they have caused the idea to be more tenaciously and violently, because more egotistically, held than ever. If some one doubts the truth of the idea it is a personal insult. A conversion to the idea is a personal triumph. At a later stage the unconscious may carry its counter-attack even further ; the crank begins to develop a secret doubt of his absolute. The doubt is consciously overcompensated, and the belief becomes fanatical. Whatever the scientific value of this account of crank mentality, the fact remains that, by whatever process, cranks do transmute opinions into absolute dogmas, which are for them substitutes for religion. I have known men whose religion was homoeopathy, others whose whole life was constellated round the faith that is anti-vivisection. The inadequacy of such ideas as surrogates of the comprehensive dogmas of religion is manifest. The crank lives narrowly and in a real sense insanely.

SUPERSTITIONS

If our original assumption is true and human nature has in fact remained fundamentally changeless throughout the historical period, then we should expect to find the contemporary world as full of superstitions as the world of the past. For superstitious beliefs and practices are the expressions of certain states of mind, and if the states of mind exist, so ought the practices and beliefs. Our age has a habit of calling itself enlightened. On what grounds it is difficult to understand, unless it regards as a progress towards enlightenment the fact that its fetishistic and magical superstitions are no longer co-ordinated with a religion, but have, so to speak, broken loose and exist in a state of independence. The Church exploited these habits of superstition and made them serve its own higher ends. Recognizing the fact that many men and women have a tendency to attribute vitality and power to inanimate objects, it supplied their needs, but with inanimate objects of a certain kind—relics, images, and the like—which served to remind the fetish-worshipper of a doctrine more intelligent and far-reaching than his own. The days of Catholic superstition are passed, and we now worship, under the name of mascots, lucky pigs, billikens, swastikas, and the like, a whole pantheon of fetishes which stand for nothing beyond themselves. No one is likely to forget how seriously these fetishes were taken during the war, what powers were then attributed to them, what genuine distress and terror were occasioned by their loss. Now that the danger is over the worship is not so ardent. But that it still persists

any one may discover who will but take the
trouble to use his eyes and ears. Of spiritual-
ism, fortune-telling, and the practice of magic
I shall say nothing. They have always existed
and they still exist, unchanged except for the
fact that there is no established religion in
relation to which these practices are bad or
good. The belief in evil spirits, though still
common, is probably less widespread than it
was, but the human tendency to hypostasize
its sense of values is still as strong as ever. Evil
spirits being out of fashion, it must therefore find
expression in other beliefs. With many people,
especially women, bacilli have taken the place
of spirits. Microbes for them are the personi-
fication of evil. They live in terror of germs
and practise elaborate antiseptic rites in order
to counteract their influence. There are mothers
who find it necessary to sterilize the handker-
chiefs that come back from the laundry ; who,
when their children scratch their finger on a
bramble, interrupt their walk and hurry home
in search of iodine ; who boil and distil the
native virtue out of every particle of food or
drink. I have known one who would not allow
her child to relieve nature anywhere but in
the open fields ; artificial retiring places were
for her infested with the evil spirits called
microbes. One is reminded irresistibly of the
ritual washings and fumigations, the incessant
preoccupation with unclean foods, unlucky days,

and inauspicious places, so common among all the primitive peoples. The forms change, but the substance remains.

PRIEST SURROGATES

The double functions of the priest, who is simultaneously ' overseer of vague things ' and doctor of souls, have been distributed in the modern priestless world, and are exercised not by one class of men but by several. In his capacity as administrator of sacraments and interpreter of the surrounding mystery the priest is now represented, inadequately enough, by the artist. The extraordinary and quite disproportionate importance attributed by the contemporary world to artists as such, regard-less of their merit, is due to the fact that the artist is the evoker of those emotional states which are the god. True, the god he evokes is often a god of the poorest quality. Consider, for example, the deity implicit in the best-selling novel or the popular ballad. Still, for those who are so constituted that they can like that sort of god, that is the sort of god they will like. There is a hierarchy both among gods and men. Those whose place in the human hierarchy is low worship gods whose place in the divine hierarchy corresponds with their own. The artist-priests who evoke low gods for low worshippers are themselves low. Still, whatever the quality of the god evoked, the artist's act is always sacramental. He does genuinely produce a god of some sort. Hence his importance in the modern world. His name is written large over the pages of *Who's Who*; hostesses ask him out to dinner; gossip writers report his doings in the press; unknown correspondents write to him about their souls, and ask him for copies of his photograph; young ladies are disposed in advance to fall in love with him. For the artist who enjoys this sort of celebrity the modern world must be a real paradise.

The priest is a confessor as well as an interpreter of mysteries. The artist can make shift to perform his sacramental functions, but he lacks the kind of training and knowledge that fits a man to be a director of conscience. It is to the lawyer and the doctor that the priest has bequeathed this part of his duties. The doctor, and especially the nerve specialist, occupies an extraordinary position in our world. His prestige was always high, even during those periods when the maladies of the spirit were regarded as being beyond his jurisdiction. Now that the exorcist is extinct and the confessor a rarity, now that psycho-therapy professes itself a science and a regular art, the doctor's prestige has been doubled. His position in the modern world is almost that of the medicine man among the primitives.

228

With the decline of priestly power the importance of the lawyer has also increased. The family solicitor takes vicarious responsibility for the acts of his clients. He is the recipient of their most intimate secrets ; he gives them not merely legal but even moral advice. Priests may disappear ; but the number of people who do not like to answer for their own actions, who shrink from making decisions and desire to be led, does not decrease. The director of conscience came into existence in response to a genuine human need. Between them, doctor and lawyer supply his vacant place.

PERSONALITY AND THE DISCONTINUITY
OF THE MIND

THE RAW MATERIALS

Heredity gives us, not a complete personality, but the materials out of which a personality can be made, and the power to make one. It gives us a body and its appetites, it gives us a set of instincts and the capacity to feel, to imagine, to reason. From these hereditary materials and from what comes to us from the ambience in which we live—our education, in the widest sense of the word, and the chances of our fate—we must construct our personality. Many are the forms that exist potentially within the yet unhewn block. Let Oldham's celebrated log bear witness.

> The workmen, still in doubt what course to take,
> Whether I'd best a saint or hog-trough make,
> After debate resolved me for a saint;
> And so famed Loyola I represent.

There is, if not a saint, at least a genuine man implicit in the raw materials with which we all set out ; and if not a hog-trough, at least a hog. What form shall be actualized is, to a great extent, within our choice. We can carve ourselves into what, within limits, we will. Within limits, I repeat. For it is obvious that the nature of the created personality must be strictly determined by the nature of the given materials. Marble temples cannot be made out of mud, though mud can be built up into a shrine and the shrine dedicated — however poor its substance and rudely inadequate its form—to the noblest of the gods. One cannot become a man of genius at will, or by having faith. The asylums are full of men who believed, more passionately even than poor Haydon, in their genius, who willed, with more consistent concentration even than Alfieri's, to be great. There are obvious limits to what may be done in the way of building up a personality. The given materials cannot be alchemically transmuted into something else ; they can only be arranged. A form may be imposed on the substance ; but the substance cannot be altered. Moreover, the nature of the psychological substance conditions to a great extent the kind of form that can be given to it, just as the nature of the granite in which they worked imposed a certain kind of artistic convention on the Egyptian sculptors, and the nature of metal an entirely different convention on the makers of Greek bronzes. It must not be imagined that a man is entirely his own artist. When he comes to the age of self-consciousness he has already been moulded by his parents, by his teachers, by all the ideals and prejudices of the society into which he happens to have been born. It may be that, when he realizes it, he will dislike the form which has been given to him during the plastic years of childhood ; it may be that he will feel impelled to remodel himself upon some different plan. Or else, if he accepts what has been done, he may continue to work at himself in the same spirit as animated the artificers of his childhood. More often he will just take himself for granted and live without troubling to inquire whether his personality is well or ill made, or if indeed his spiritual substance has been given any organized form at all.

I have been taking it for granted up till now that the personality is not given, but requires to be constructed by each individual (or for him by others) out of the hereditary and environmental materials at his disposal. It is time now to justify this assumption by an appeal to the observable peculiarities of man's nature, to show that what is given by heredity (which is all we need discuss, since the environment is obviously not a personality) is not originally an ordered whole, but something much more like chaos, requiring to be moulded and, to use the language of the schools, *informed* in accordance with some principle of design.

WORDSWORTH AND NATURE

The chaotic nature of the elements from which a personality must be made has always been recognized. Here is Wordsworth's account of them and of the process by which they are co-ordinated :

> Dust as we are, the immortal spirit grows
> Like harmony in music ; there is a dark
> Inscrutable workmanship that reconciles
> Discordant elements, makes them cling together
> In one society.   How strange that all
> The terrors, pains, and early miseries,
> Regrets, vexations, lassitudes interfused
> Within my mind should e'er have borne a part,
> And that a needful part, in making up
> The calm existence that is mine when I
> Am worthy of myself.

The lines are noble ; but the beauty of the language must not blind us to the defect in the ideas which it expresses.   Wordsworth, so at least it seems to me, attributes too great a part in the making of the personality to the ' dark inscrutable workmanship ' of Nature in the sense of an external and providential power, too little to the deliberate artistry of the individual himself and the formative influences of his education.   In the present essay I hope to show that the personality ' which is ours when we are worthy of ourselves ' is a product of our own and of other deliberate human efforts ; that the desirable end can be, ought to be, and is achieved by man himself and not, in Wordsworth's words, ' thanks to the means which Nature deigned to employ.'   Nature or Providence (call the external powers by what name you will) may play its part But the gods help only those who help themselves. With an almost Islamic piety Wordsworth shifts the whole burden of responsibility on to the shoulders of Providence. ' It was the doing of Allah,' he seems to say. ' Blessed be the name of Allah.' But to a Westerner and an individualist such piety seems rather immoral—an excuse for laziness and the avoidance of responsibility—and the explanation of events by their final and supernatural causes is a piece of facile profundity which strikes us as merely uninteresting. Of Nature's part in the moulding of a personality I shall say nothing, for the good reason that nothing can be clearly said. The goddess, Nature, is as unknowable as any other deity, and her works are as mysterious. Man's part in the business is my theme. Man's part, not Nature's. It has the advantage of being observable, a proper study, and not ineffable.

METAPHORS

That one should have to talk about the mind in metaphors is unfortunate, but inevitable. Neither common nor scientific language provides us with an idiom in which the nature and workings of the spirit can be adequately described. It is hardly possible to say anything about it except by metaphors and similes borrowed from

234

the material world which we can see and touch. I have spoken up till now as though the hereditarily given psychological materials were so much clay for a sculptor to mould into a form, so much rubble and masonry to be built up by the architect into a house. And in so far as this simile emphasized the raw chaotic nature of what is given, and the importance in the process of its conversion into a personality of something like artistic treatment, it served well enough. But architecture and sculpture exist in space, and are the same at different moments of time. Human beings inhabit time as well as space, and vary from moment to moment. The hereditarily given materials of a personality are chaotic in time, not in space. The stones out of which the architect will make his house lie scattered in space. The psychological materials out of which the individual must construct his personality are discontinuous in time. In order to create a personality one must discover some principle of continuity, one must devise an ideal framework in which the naturally discontinuous materials can be harmoniously fitted. Temporal gaps separate the elements of a personality from one another ; the framework should span these gulfs of time ; the principle of continuity should act as a kind of cement in which the time-divided elements are set.

DISCONTINUITIES

The body is perpetually changing its material substance ; but it persists, unmistakably, as the same individual body throughout life. This is a fact which causes us to attribute a persistent personality to people who, psychologically speaking, have little or no personality, being to all intents and purposes spiritually discontinuous. The body, I repeat, persists ; but its activity is not uniformly regular ; it is undulatory and tide-like. Our bodies function rhythmically, and the rhythms are numerous and varied. Some, like respiration and the beating of the heart, are rapid ; others, like the recurrent need for sleep and nourishment, are almost as regular, but slower. Others, again, like the periodical return of sexual appetite, are more irregular, since they depend on physiological processes, whose rapidity varies from individual to individual, and also in the same individual according to his state of health, his environment, and the habits he has formed. Others are still more irregular and still slower, for they depend on the way in which our bodies react to the cosmic environment, to seasonal changes of temperature, seasonal variations in the amount of sunshine, and the kind of nourishment taken. Imposed on these more or less regular rhythms are a whole series of quite irregular fluctuations in the body's activity. Thus, slight illness and accident produce temporary derangements of the normal physiological life. If they are chronic and severe, the derangement is permanent and the mind is compelled to adapt itself to a new physiological environment.

These irregular fluctuations in the body's activity, together with a certain number of the regular rhythmical variations, have a direct effect on the accompanying mind, which reacts to the physiological changes by passing from one state into another, distinct from and discontinuous with the first. Thus, the state of mind of a man who is very hungry is radically different from that of a man who has just eaten a large meal, a fact of which every subordinate with a favour to ask or a shortcoming to be forgiven, every wife in need of a new dress, every son with an examination failure to report, has always taken advantage. Tolerance and kindliness are the spiritual concomitants of a full stomach. Hunger breeds irritability and rancour, personal anxiety and a pessimistic outlook on the world. Between the state of mind of a man at five minutes to one, before his lunch, and at half-past, when he is helping himself to cheese, a great gulf is fixed. The two states are discontinuous.

The rhythm of the body's sexual life affects the mind no less strikingly than do the rhythms of its hunger. A man with an unslaked sexual

appetite is quite unlike the same man immediately after satisfaction.

> Enjoyed no sooner, but despisèd straight,
> Past reason hunted, but no sooner had,
> Past reason hated . . .

Shakespeare might have referred to the satiated
man's feeling of repentance ; to his good resolu-
tions ; to that mood of melancholy virtue in
which the spectacle, the mere thought of lasciviousness seems so profoundly shocking ; to that
high moral attitude which the satiated lecher
so often adopts towards the still unsatiated ; to
the calm which in all cases succeeds the frenzy
of yet unappeased appetite.

The body's responses to the seasonal changes
in its external environment can rarely, in the
nature of things, be so violent as its responses
to those very considerable disturbances in its
equilibrium, felt as hunger or sexual appetite.
But though not violent, they are sufficiently
well marked to have attracted attention from
the earliest times. Recent studies on the physiological effects of sunlight and temperature have
explained, in part at any rate, the mechanism
of seasonal bodily changes. The mind responds
to these bodily changes, and is at the same
time directly affected by the spectacle which
the various seasons offer. The result is the
production of those typical seasonal states of
mind which Thomas Hardy has so often and so

well described. There are days in May when
it is literally impossible for any person with
health and leisure enough to walk into the
country to believe in determinism, original sin,
or the ultimate futility of all existence. There
are days in autumn and winter when it is all
but impossible not to believe in these things.
There is a discontinuity between the seasonal
states of mind. A similar discontinuity is to be
found between the state of mind of a man
living in the tropics and the state of mind of
the same man living in a temperate climate.

The way in which bodily illness can affect the
mind is well known. Biliousness begets irritability and depression ; its philosophical con-
comitant is intense pessimism or violent world
hatred. Constipation is accompanied by a less
extreme form of the same philosophy. Malaria
produces an intimate conviction of the vanity
of life and the futility of all human effort.
Epileptics often pass through moments of in-
enarrable ecstasy which may give a sense and
a value to their whole life. Of the same nature
are the ' anaesthetic revelations ' of those who
have been put to sleep with laughing gas, and
the artificial raptures of the addicts to ether,
alcohol, opium, cocaine, and all the other drugs
which act on the mind through the body.
Bodily accidents involving disablement or dis-
figurement affect the mind by creating a painful
sense of inferiority. This inferiority is either

accepted, in which case the victim shrinks into his shell and hides from his fellows as though he feared them ; or else it is violently over-compensated, and a truculent, aggressive atti-tude is adopted towards the world. The effects of such accidents on the body are generally permanent, so that the state of mind which they produce is also permanent. In slight re-current illnesses the mind passes frequently from one state to another and back again. There is a discontinuity between, for example, the eupeptic and the dyspeptic states of mind, between sober and drunken, normal and epileptic states.

MENTAL INTERMITTENCE

I have spoken up till now of those mental discontinuities whose cause is predominantly physiological. But bodily changes are not the only sources of discontinuity, which may also be determined by purely psychological causes. State succeeds distinct and different state, not because of any abnormal alteration in the physio-logical environment of the mind, but because that happens to be the way in which the mind works.

In his volume on ' the intermittences of the heart ' Marcel Proust has patiently described and analysed the way in which emotions come and go, as though endowed with a life of their own independent of the life of the whole being. The grief which his hero did not feel at the time of his grandmother's death suddenly overwhelms him months later, when a casual gesture reminds him of her. From one moment to the next the state of his mind radically changes. There is a discontinuity between the person as he was before making the gesture and the same person as he was after making it. Owing to the important part which association plays in our mental life, discontinuities of this kind are very common. A perfume, a melody, the view of some object can transport our mind out of the present into the past, can reproduce in us the emotions which we felt on some previous occasion, the thoughts which then occurred to us—thoughts and emotions which are often entirely irrelevant to the present situation, but which impose themselves upon us in what seems sometimes an almost violent and tyrannical fashion.

The relations subsisting between the unconscious and the conscious mind are obscure. But there seems to be little doubt that one of the offices of the unconscious is to act, so to speak, as trimmer in the boat of life. When the conscious mind leans too far in one direction, the tendency of the unconscious is to lean in the opposite direction so as to restore the vital balance, which the conscious mind, if unrestrained, would fatally destroy. Thus it

frequently happens that people who devote themselves in a consciously unselfish manner to the
service of an ideal or principle, develop the
most pettily egoistic and rancorous feelings.
They become oversensitive and morbidly suspicious, regarding all criticisms, however dis-
passionate, of the cause which they serve as
being malevolently directed against themselves
and inspired by the basest personal motives.
Suppressed in the conscious mind, which is
occupied exclusively with its noble and disinterested cause, the personal, self-regarding tendencies ' get their own back ' in the unconscious.
The unconscious state of mind is in contradiction
with the conscious, and when the two states
alternate, there is psychological discontinuity.
Many other examples might be cited of conflict
between the conscious and unconscious attitude, resulting in the same sort of discontinuity.
Thus we frequently observe that the consciously convinced puritan is deeply preoccupied
in his unconscious mind with precisely those
sexual matters which he professes to hate.
Another example is that of the man with a
consciously formulated scientific outlook on
parts at least of the physical universe. Pro-
fessed men of science are often extremely superstitious and credulous about matters lying
outside their own particular province. This
may be explained on the hypothesis that the
religious feelings, which are ignored by the

conscious mind when dealing with the subjects in which it is predominantly interested, tend to flourish all the more rankly in the unconscious. Making irruptions into the light of day, they manifest themselves in strange superstitions and a childish credulity with regard to all matters except those which the conscious mind has elected or been taught to consider through scientific spectacles. In this last case the compensatory action of the unconscious is greatly facilitated by our present system of education, which insists on the strictly objective and matter-of-fact treatment of non-human nature, while reserving the right to deal with every human activity in accordance with subjective criteria. Brought up from childhood to think materialistically about one set of phenomena, idealistically and even mystically about another, we find ourselves quite naturally adopting one mental attitude at one moment and a different attitude, quite incompatible with the first, at another. Inconsistency is almost forced on us ; we are compelled to live our intellectual life discontinuously.

THE FRAMEWORKS OF PERSONALITY

It is out of such naturally discrete and separate elements that each individual has to build up his personality—to compose it (for the musical metaphor is the more apt) so that the discontinuous states may reveal themselves as part of a whole, developing in time. The most perfect personality is that in which the natural discords are harmonized by some principle of unity, in which the discontinuous psychological elements are fitted into a framework of purposive ideals strong enough to bridge the gaps between them. Systems of morality, ideals, codes of honour exist to provide the individual with ready - made frameworks. They serve well enough for those who do not object to wearing other people's clothes and are not particular about a perfect fit. The more fastidious and self-conscious will prefer to construct their own framework—out of traditional materials, no doubt, but selected and personally re-created, not blindly accepted in the form in which tradition offers them. Making a framework is something that sounds easy enough ; but it is not. The number of completely unified personalities is small. Most of us go through life incompletely unified—part person, the rest a mere collection of discontinuous psychological elements. For example, there are many people who permit their sexual activities to exist in almost complete independence of the rest of their beings. Appetite grows, a particular state of mind is induced ; appetite is satisfied, another state of mind is induced. And the process repeats itself in a world apart from that of the intellect, the feelings, the imagination, the creative and directed will.

All these psychological elements may be co-
ordinated by some unifying principle, may be
held together in some purposive ideal framework which remains unaffected by the discontinuity of successive mental states. The
individual is a personality with regard to everything but sex, which is left detached to lead a
more or less completely independent life of its
own. This state of psychological affairs has often
been recommended, explicitly or by implication,
as the most suitable for practical life. Its most
eminent champion in recent times was Anatole
France. France, it is true, justified his conception of sex as mere detached appetite by
that same Reason which served as the unifying
principle of his other vital activities. Like his
eighteenth-century predecessors, France found
it reasonable to regard sex as a simple physiological function and love-making as scarcely
more than a medicinable act of purging. The
only possible comment is : If this be reason,
then let me be irrational. A reason that con-
demns a man to forgo the experiences resulting from the co-ordination of his sexual with
his intellectual and imaginative activities is
something that makes for a reduction, not an
increase of life. France's solution of the sexual
problem is almost as unsatisfactory as the solution offered by the Christian ascetics at whose
expense he was always amusing himself. In
the ascetics a certain amount of that sexual

energy which the practice of chastity preserved intact was sometimes transmuted into intellectual, imaginative, and devotional energy. The 'unprejudiced' who live their sexual life exclusively on the physiological plane simply get rid of the energy as it accumulates. In the ascetics, it is true, this energy was often deflected and became malevolent and self-destructive ; often, but not always. In the rationalists of France's type it is never allowed to become destructive ; but equally it never has a chance of becoming beneficently effective. It is just consumed on the physiological plane, while the intellectual, emotional, and imaginative life goes on, so to speak, in an upper storey. To co-ordinate sex with the other activities of life, to incorporate it organically in the whole personality, is certainly difficult. Moreover, propitious circumstances must conspire with individual effort. It takes two to make, not only a quarrel, but its amorous opposite. Where some malignant chance withholds the second person's necessary co-operation, individual effort is not of much use. But when the necessary circumstances are given, how amply worth the making !

PROUST

The most curious feature of Proust's mentality is his complacent acceptance of the 'intermittences of the heart' and all the other psychological discontinuities which he so subtly and exhaustively describes. He offers us a picture of human nature in the raw, so to speak, without ever suggesting how the crude material should be worked up, without even hinting that it should be worked up or that he himself had ever attempted to do so. No author has studied the intermittences of the spirit with so much insight and patience, and none has shown himself so placidly content to live the life of an intermittent being. A scientific voluptuary of the emotions, Proust seems to have had no ambition to do more than know himself; the idea of using his knowledge in order to make himself better never seems to have occurred to him. There is a strange moral poverty about his book. He offers us the subtlest of psychological analyses, but never suggests what we ought to do when we have achieved the self-knowledge made possible by his insight. The end of life, it is implied, is to allow psychological events to happen to one and to know how and why they happen, in order to be able to savour their quality with a more conscious enjoyment. This may be all very well for a retired invalid like Proust; but for those whose life is mainly passed out of the sickroom it is hardly a satisfactory philosophy. The man who would face the world with a complete and consistently effective personality cannot resign himself to his discontinuity. He cannot permit himself to be one man before lunch and another after ; to be here at one moment, and the next, at the whim of some chance suggestion, in another place and time, another intellectual and emotional atmosphere. He cannot afford to be at one moment ' perjured, murderous, bloody, full of blame,' and the next, when appetite has been assuaged, a disgusted (and disgusting) moralist. He cannot allow the weather, or his bowels, or his bank account to dictate his philosophy of life ; and if, beneficently, some physiological accident should seem to reveal the secrets of remoter truth, he must be able to make sense of the apocalypse, to find a place for it in his total scheme. It is indispensable for him to have some unifying principle that shall preserve him identical with himself through all the changes in the outward and inward environment of his mind. He must create for himself a moral framework that shall persist in spite of the fluctuations that go on within it, a framework strong enough to carry the person he desires to be across those gaps of time when nature, if he abandoned himself to nature, would make him play another and an unacceptable part.

THE NATURE OF THE FRAMEWORKS

In the course of history men have invented many frameworks of continuity in which to arrange the naturally discrete and separate elements of a possible personality. There have been philosophical and religious frameworks, artistic frameworks and practical business frameworks. Men belonging to different types have chosen different frameworks. But at any given period there is one kind of framework which predominates, there is one orthodox principle of continuity, which is generally a religion with its traditional code of morality. A framework is valuable in so far as it makes possible the creation of a complete and harmonious personality. We must know the end before we can assess the worth of the means for its achievement. The perfect personality is one in which all the psychological elements are taken account of and exploited. Nothing in such a personality is suppressed, or rather (since an element of the mind can no more be suppressed than an organ of the body) nothing is relegated to a lower sphere or pushed into the darkness of unconsciousness. Instinctive tendencies, which if they were allowed to exist in independence would be socially undesirable and disruptive of the personality, are harnessed, so to speak, and made to spend their energy in forwarding the co-ordinated activities of the whole spirit. The intermittences of the mind and its capacity for irrelevance are admitted ; but these defects are made to provide their own remedy. The man who would co-ordinate his personality must devise a technique for association-making. Only in this way can he compel the powers, or rather the weaknesses, that make for mental discontinuity to work in the cause of a deliberately chosen continuity.

> My heart leaps up when I behold
> A rainbow in the sky.

We cannot produce rainbows at will; but we can deliberately put the mind in contact with other things and thoughts that happen for us to be charged with associations, in such a way that the days, yes, and the hours and minutes, shall not be discontinuous, but ' bound each to each by natural piety.'

The perfect personality provides us with a standard by which to judge the frameworks which society offers, ready-made, to its individual members. A good framework is one which has room for all the psychological elements of a personality. The more the framework leaves out, the fewer the elements which the principle of continuity co-ordinates, the worse they are. Judged by this standard, the existing frameworks, the accepted principles of continuity, are far from adequate—much less adequate than that which they have replaced. For the old Catholic framework was wonderfully comprehensive. It found room for reason and for emotion, for intuition and imagination. The disruptive forces of sex were given a cosmic significance and canalized, not quite adequately perhaps, within the system. The invention of chivalrous and platonic love provided a compromise between asceticism and indulgence, and a method for harnessing the instinct to thought and emotion. A supernatural sense and meaning were given to life, a sense and a meaning in the light of which it was possible for the individual to see all his acts in due proportion. By means of ritual and constantly repeated ceremonies, of innumerable images and symbols, that victim of association, the naturally wandering and discontinuous mind of man, was compelled at every moment to remember the supernatural meaning of life, and remembering, to shape its thoughts accordingly. It was in regard to men's natural tendencies towards violence and avarice that the Catholic system showed itself least successful. The conception of chivalry was, it is true, a real principle of unity, co-ordinating natural ferocity with the rest of the mind in a way which, at the time it was invented, could not have been improved. But with the better organization of government and the consequent increase of orderliness, with the progress of invention and the resulting modifications in the art of war, the idea of military chivalry became obsolete and died out. But the natural tendencies towards violence did not die, and the Church devised no new principle of unification to co-ordinate these instinctive impulses with the rest of the mind. It merely tried to suppress them. Infected with the heresy of humanity-worship, the feebler and less realistic religions pretended that these unpleasant instincts did not exist. The instincts refused to play the game and went on existing. In athletics our contemporaries have discovered a means by which intrinsically dangerous tendencies can be given harmless expression and made to serve, not oppose, the interests of morality. Fair play is the chivalry by which the mimic war of games (the, for most men, sufficient substitute for genuine butcher's work) is co-ordinated with the higher activities of the mind.

The mediaeval Church never succeeded in finding an economic chivalry to transform and spiritualize the covetousness of its children. Men learned to fight like Christians ; but it was like the Jews of fable that they did business. The investigations of Mr. Tawney and the other historians of economic policy have shown what strenuous efforts were made by the Church to control and keep in check the acquisitive instincts. In vain. All attempts to moralize covetousness by teaching that money is only held in trust, that the rich have duties and responsibilities as well as rights, entirely failed. The acquisitive instincts refused to be co-ordinated with the rest of the mind. More-over, they proved too strong to be checked.

By the beginning of the eighteenth century the Church had resigned itself to impotence ; religion was one thing, but business was business.

THE MODERN FRAMEWORK

The decay of the organized religions has meant that the majority of men and women no longer build themselves up into personalities within the Catholic framework. The modern framework—or rather frameworks, for there are several of them, but with a family likeness among themselves—is much less comprehensive than that which it has ousted. It is a framework in which only certain elements of the mind are able to find a place. The others are left out, to lead an obscure rebellious life in independence of the organized personality. But before describing the activities of these mutinous outcasts, let me show what psychological elements have been included within the modern framework, and for what reason.

The unifying principle by means of which the moderns have tried to co-ordinate the elements of man's nature into a personality is social efficiency. Life no longer has a supernatural significance ; the point of living is to achieve that natural, that all too natural, consummation—socially recognized success. It is in the name of this success that the discontinuities in man's spiritual life are to be bridged, the separate elements of his nature co-ordinated, and its discords harmonized. Those mental functions are esteemed which make for socially recognized success ; those which militate against efficiency are despised, and at the same time dreaded. No use can be found for them in a personality which it has been decided in advance is to be the personality of a socially efficient and successful being. They must be forcibly suppressed, or else treated as the Christian Scientist and the proverbial ostrich treat all the realities they find unpleasant. If these particular unpleasant realities refuse to believe you when you tell them that they do not exist —well, so much the worse for you and your prospects of achieving success.

Socially recognized success is professional success ; a man imposes himself on society by doing well at his work. The qualities required to achieve success in most professions are qualities of the reason, the will, and the intuition. The successful man must be able to think clearly, to concentrate his attention and prevent his mind from wandering, to work hard even when he is feeling disinclined to work. That is to say, that his powers of reason and of will must be highly developed. In many professions intuition, which is the faculty of unconscious perception, the power of seeing beyond the immediate sensuous superficialities of here and now, of detecting realities behind masks, and dynamic possibilities latent in the stolid present, is hardly less indispensable than reason or will. No one who lacks intuition can hope to achieve success in any profession in which it is part of his business to deal directly and personally with men and women, or to speculate on the future. Under the present dispensation these qualities of reason, will, and intuition are at a premium, because they and they alone can guarantee that professional success, the achievement of which has become the desirable end that gives to life its whole significance and point. Among the other psychological elements which have been co-ordinated in the modern success-per-sonality, the most important are the acquisitive tendencies. These have been moralized not by any process of sublimation, but by a simple reversal of values. What was previously black is now called white. Covetousness, which was a deadly sin in the days of our mediaeval ancestors, is now one of the cardinal virtues. By this means a source of what was once most inconvenient energy has been harnessed and made to do work within the organized person-ality. Whether we are right in reckoning as a virtue what our ancestors called a sin is another question. It is true that by doing so we have made the tendencies in question seem, tempor-arily at any rate, less troublesome. But the spiritual peace has been bought at a price—a price which we are already paying, and which our children will continue to pay long after the precarious respite which it purchased has become a matter of ancient history.

I have already mentioned our modern successes in co-ordinating the natural tendencies towards violence. The organization of athletics as a substitute for bloodier encounters, the social consecration of athletic success, and the harnessing of games to morality are notable achievements. By comparison, our failure to deal adequately with sex or the emotions seems all the more striking. Neither sex nor the emotions make for professional success. Indeed, they often militate against it. Our method of dealing with sex is still the traditional Catholic method. But there were transcendental reasons for the Catholic institutions of matrimony and celibacy. We have no such reasons. The best that we can say is that moderation in sexual matters is desirable, because any intemperance in the way of love or lust interferes with our capacity for doing business, any infringement of the commonly accepted code is a handicap in the race for success. It is the same with the emotions. There is very little professional use for feeling. Hence the revival of that strange idea of the Stoics, that feeling is somehow intrinsically unmanly, that it is an inferior function of the mind which ought in all circumstances to be suppressed. From the eighteenth century onwards, with only a few brief intermissions, the purely reasonable has been the ideal man. The feelings have been exiled into an outer darkness, apart from and below the personality co-ordinated by the principle of success. The attempt to co-ordinate the discontinuous emotions, to press them into the service of some cause superior to themselves, has practically ceased. The very devices by which the Church contrived to lead the wayward mind and harmonize its discordant states have fallen into decay. Our streets are no longer crowded with the pageantry of suggestive ceremonial ; the sight of symbol and image no longer reminds us of the mysterious meaning of life, no longer compels us to think and feel along a single set of channels. Not only has the ritual of organized religion disappeared from out of our world ; all the lay ceremonial of ordinary life is fast vanishing. Mourning and feasting, good manners and etiquette, the observance of fast days and holy days—all the ritual of natural piety is dying out. Governments, it is true, still use suggestive symbols in order to crystallize a little of men's exuberant feelings in the form of patriotism. The world is full of flags—a little too full for some tastes. It is still fuller, however, of advertisements. Man's suggestibility and his habit of remembering in terms of associations were once exploited by the Church to the end that man might build himself up—poor heap of scattered elements !—

PROPER STUDIES

into a personality. They are exploited now by tradesmen to the end that advertisers may become rich.

Outlawed, the unco-ordinated instincts and emotions do not thereby cease to exist ; they live on, but apart, and as it were autonomously. The rationalizing Stoic leads his barbarous one-sided life of reason ; every now and then the outlaw breaks in on him and he finds himself swept off his feet by grotesque passions, tempted into sordid vices, infected by the strangest superstitions, the most maudlin sentimentalities, giving way to the most petty egoisms. The youngest generation does not even attempt to be stoical. Co-ordinated for success, its members (not all of course, but how many !) know that reason, will, intuition, and covetousness are the only valuable elements of the mind. But though the other elements are for them of no account, they do not for that reason attempt to suppress them altogether. They admit their existence, and more than that, they abandon themselves deliberately in their leisure moments to the caprices of the outlaws. Sex and emotions in them are unco-ordinated ; they exist, so to speak, in the raw. In so far as they are sexual and emotional beings, the youngest of our contemporaries seem to be entirely uncivilized. And they admit their savagery in these matters, they abandon themselves to it. ' Savagery ' is perhaps the wrong word ; for savages are co-ordinated within a rigid framework of taboos. Our modern savages have no taboos of any sort. They copulate with the casual promiscuousness of dogs ; they make use of every violent emotion-producing sensation for its own sake, because it gives a momentary thrill. In the discontinuity of their emotional states they find like Proust (who for all his refinement is in this respect a primitive), not something to be deplored and as far as possible corrected, but something curious and entertaining. They pass from state to mental state with the enjoyment of children visiting the side-shows of a fair. In one booth is lasciviousness, in the next disgust. You pay your money and you take your choice of drunken fury or drunken sentimentality. The naturally discontinuous states are left unco-ordinated. No attempt is made to link up sex and feelings with the organized personality. Indeed, as we have seen, they cannot be linked up with a personality co-ordinated for social success. The entire irrelevance of these outlawed elements is what, precisely, constitutes their charm for people out for a ' good time,' and determined not to accept any responsibility for their own actions.

A NOTE ON IDEALS

THE TANGENT AND THE CURVE

The earth, if left to itself, would move in a straight line through the heavens. It happens, however, to exist in the neighbourhood of the sun, and so is compelled to travel in an ellipse. If the sun were suddenly to lose its attractive force, the earth would cease to move round it, and would fly off in a straight line tangential to the curve it had been describing under the influence of gravitation. The earth is not a conscious being ; but if it were, we might be justified in saying that at any given moment it was trying to fly off at a tangent, but that its desire was perpetually thwarted by the action of the more powerful sun ; its actual course is the product of its own tangential yearning and the sun's attraction. There is an allegory, as Pareto has shown in an expressive illustration, to be discovered here. The ideal is situated on the tangent. Man strains towards it ; but the forces of the world in which he lives unsleepingly act upon him. It is impossible for him to move along the tangent to the desired goal. The product of his tangential desire and of the forces which act on him is his real course through time. The fact that the earth moves must not make us imagine that man's course is always a progress in the modern political sense. The product of his ideal yearning and the forces acting on him may be, not a process of change, but a static condition. In China and India, for example, ideals and natural forces combine to produce social fixity, not progress. The two forces compensate one another ; an equilibrium is reached. A similar balancing of forces must be achieved before anything like regular and steady progress can be kept up. If the forces are not balanced, movement becomes irregular and catastrophic. The earth describes a regular ellipse because, speaking anthropomorphically, it desires to move along that one particular straight line which can be drawn tangential to the curve at the particular point where at any given moment it happens to be. If it desired to reach a point not situated on the tangent of the moment, its course, which is the product of its desire and of the forces acting upon it, would not be regularly elliptical. Something analogous happens in the microcosmic sphere. When men propose to themselves an ideal which is not merely unrealizable (all good ideas are unrealizable), but actually impossible, because having no relation to the realities of life in the given place and time, the product of their efforts to reach it and of the forces acting upon them will not be a progress or a stationary equilibrium, but an irregular movement off the line of humanly possible advance. For example, the ideal of communism in property and women is an impossible ideal ; for it is an ideal which is not, so to speak, tangential to man's actual position, or to any point which he has ever occupied in human history. The average man has at all times been keenly interested in private property and marriage, and no ideal which denies the existence of such an interest can be pursued with profit. The democratic ideal is situated partly on a tangent to the actual human position, partly off it. The part of the democratic doctrine which affirms that all men should be given equal opportunities to develop whatever powers they may possess is an ideal, if not finally and absolutely realizable, at least possible. For it denies no facts ; on the contrary it draws attention to facts previously unnoticed—to the talents, that is to say, which are latent in exceptional individuals of every social class—and inculcates the duty of permitting these facts to see the light and be made use of. But the doctrine of democracy has another chapter. Not only are men to be given equal opportunity to develop their faculties ; they are also to be treated, in certain circumstances at any rate, as though their faculties were equal. Where politics are concerned, it is to be assumed that human beings have equal abilities. (It is significant that the practical sense of men and women should have revolted

262

against the application of this doctrine to matters which they feel to be of more immediate and personal interest than politics. All are equally fit to rule, but all are most certainly not equally fit to keep accounts or manage a business.) The ideal of political democracy, that all men ought to participate in ruling their country, is off the tangent ; for the assumption on which it is based is untrue. The abilities of men are demonstrably not equal. The product of men's efforts to reach this misplaced ideal and of the forces, external and psychological, which act upon them, has been a very uncertain movement which only the most blindly enthusiastic democrats could call progressive. The rise of Fascism and of its equivalents beyond the frontiers of Italy is an eloquent comment on the ideal of political democracy.

GOOD AND BAD IDEALS

The most valuable ideals are possible, but unrealizable. Such ideas are framed so as not to contradict the facts of human nature ; their pursuit does not involve the denial by individuals or societies of any fundamental reality. They are at the same time unrealizable, so that the incentive to pursue them never fails. A realizable ideal (which must also, it is obvious, be a possible one, involving no denial of facts) is not so valuable as an unrealizable one. And the more easily realizable, the less valuable it is. For a realizable ideal is not situated on a tangent to the curve of human development ; it is on the curve itself, immediately in front, and within reach, of the person or the society which formulated the ideal. Or, to be more precise, it is situated at a point through which the curve would pass if the idealist were trying to move along a tangent, and were being at the same time acted upon by other forces. In actual fact the curve will not run through that point precisely because the ideal is situated on the curve and not outside on a tangent to it. Progressive movement is the product of tangential yearning and the action of external forces. By making his ideal too easily realizable the idealist is giving to all the forces that are external to his ideal-directed will the power to deflect him from the progressive course. A man with no ideal would be simply at the mercy of the forces acting on him. A man with a possible but unrealizable ideal makes as much progress as is consistent with the real existence of the forces external to his will. The man with the impossible and unrealizable ideal comes to grief by trying, not to use the external forces, but to go against them. The man with the possible and too easily realizable ideal uses the external forces, but permits himself to be carried away by them to an extent that does not befit a being capable of formulating ideals and of voluntarily pursuing them.

The contemporary world is full of ideals that are too easily realizable. There is, for example, that ideal of social success which is now, as I have tried to show in another essay, so widely used as a unifying principle to co-ordinate the discrete and discontinuous elements of the personality. How inadequately it serves this purpose I have already shown. The individual who uses the ideal of social success as a co-ordinating framework finds himself with a personality from which some of the most important of the hereditarily given psychological materials are excluded. Inadequate as a principle of co-ordination, the ideal of success is also too easily realizable. A realized ideal ceases to be an incentive to further advance. The man who has attained his ideal goal achieves at the same time a belief in the vanity of all things. It is difficult for those whose ideal has been success to become successful without at the same time becoming cynical. Success and cynicism are not only achieved ; they are also inherited. For in societies like ours, where success is regarded as a rational ideal, people whose parents happen to be rich and influential are born with the ideals which tradition invites them to accept already realized. Unless they can find some more adequate and unrealizable ideal to pursue, they are condemned to cynicism from the cradle. As an incentive to social improvement this ideal is no less inadequate. For if you believe in success, you must believe in the society in relation to which you are successful. Society must remain static in order that individuals may move securely upwards within it ; it must persist in order that the results of that upward movement may be enjoyed.

DEGENERATION OF IDEALS

Ideals which in the past were tangential and unrealizable have been transformed in the modern world into realizable ideals. The old and hallowed names have been preserved, but their significance has been radically altered. As originally formulated, the Christian ideal of service was possible but unrealizable. It is only too realizable now. For service, in our Americanized world, is simply efficient business. If you supply a public demand efficiently and cheaply—a demand, it may be added, which you yourself have largely created by means of advertisement—then you are doing service. Christian service is a matter of humility, self-devotion, and charity. The qualities required of the contemporary servants of society are simply business acumen and the indispensable minimum of conventional honesty. Modern business organizers seem to take their ideal of service very seriously. They fill their advertisements with sanctimonious phrases. For the benefit of their employees they publish grandiloquent accounts of the Firm's activities (the Firm or

House is always spelt with a capital letter, as though it were a divine entity), showing how efficiently and with what Christian devotion it serves the world. They train their children up in the belief that business is religion. ' I am convinced,' says one of their most eloquent preachers, Mr. Glen Buck of Chicago, ' that almost the finest achievement of mankind is the very tangible thing that we call American business. For the first time in history the foremost activities of a great nation are running in parallels with the on-sweeping ideals of the world's straightest thinking. Our business intelligence has so far outgrown our political intelligence that it looms like a white lily on a stagnant pool. In the stress of the honest day's work we have at last convincingly demonstrated that true efficiency and high ethical standards are inseparable. And the result is a moral achievement almost unmatched in time.' ' Ethics,' writes the same author, ' would take a backward step if advertizing were suppressed.' ' To be a shopkeeper is to have the opportunity to be of substantial human service through self-developing experience.' ' Business is the means by which science is making of itself a mighty human service.' ' America's wealth has been a high contributing factor to the process that has made her the most spiritually minded nation that has ever turned its face to the sun.' Mr. Buck and his colleagues are so richly and emphatically aphoristic that one is tempted to go on quoting indefinitely. But the temptation must be resisted ; there is not ' world enough and time ' for more quotations, however admirable. Those I have given are sufficient to illustrate very clearly the modern tendency to make ideals realizable, to remove them from their place on the tangent to a new position on the curve within easy reach of the idealist. The religions which once provided men with their ideals have lost their power. Most people at the present time have no religion, only a substitute or surrogate, which stands to religion in the relation of custard powder to eggs, and roasted corn to coffee. The religion of business is one of these substitutes. It is, up to a point, a good substitute. A great many people have been able to persuade themselves, temporarily at any rate, that making money is a noble and essentially spiritual act, and that the highest type of humanity is the average man. The belief serves to give significance to an existence which, in the absence of a religious explanation of the world, seems entirely pointless ; it provides an ideal incentive to action and justifies philosophically what would otherwise be a life of mere appetite and habit. But the defects of the religion of business are manifest. To begin with, it does not accord with experience ; for there are acts which every human being intuitively feels to be spiritually

better than money-making ; there are men who
are immediately recognized by all their fellows
as incomparably superior to the average man.
The ideal of business service is merely a justification for social success. You become successful
by serving, you are virtuous because you make
money. But when success has been achieved
and money made, the ideal has been realized ;
and when the ideal is realized, the world, for
any man who stops for a moment to think,
becomes a thing of vanity. The alternatives
are either not to think, but just continue to
chatter and rush about as though you were
doing something enormously important, or else
to think, admit the world's vanity and live
cynically. Sooner or later the shallow and
untrue philosophy of business and the all too
realizable ideals of social success must infallibly
land their devotees on the horns of this dilemma.

INSANE IDEALS

A madman is one whose way of thinking and
acting does not conform with that of the majority
of his contemporaries. Sanity is a matter of
statistics. What most men do at any given
place and period is the sane and normal thing
to do. This is the definition of sanity on which
we base our social practice. For us, here and
now, the many are sane, the few mad. But
here-and-now judgments are in their nature
provisional and relative. What seems sanity to

us because it is the behaviour of the many may seem *sub specie aeternitatis* a madness. Nor is it necessary to invoke eternity as a witness. History is sufficient. The self-styled sane majority at any given moment may appear to the historian, who has studied the thoughts and actions of the innumerable dead, a tiny handful of lunatics. Considering the matter from another view-point, the psychologist may reach the same conclusion. The mind, he knows, consists of such-and-such elements, which exist and must be taken account of. If a man tries to live as though certain of these constituent elements of his being did not exist, he is trying to live, in an absolute psychological sense, abnormally. He is trying to be mad ; and to try to be mad is insanity.

Applying these two tests, the historian's and the psychologist's, to the sane majority of the contemporary West, what do we find ? We find that the ideals and the philosophy of life now generally accepted are quite unlike the ideals and philosophy accepted at almost all other periods. Mr. Buck and the millions for whom he speaks are overwhelmingly in the minority. The countless dead pass judgment on them ; they are mad. The psychologists confirm their verdict. Success—'the bitch-goddess, Success,' in William James's phrase — demands strange sacrifices from those who worship her. Nothing short of spiritual self-mutilation can secure her favours. The man co-ordinated for success is one who has been forced to leave half his spirit outside his personality. And if he accepts the ideals and the philosophy of life which the bitch-goddess has to offer, he finds himself condemned either to strenuous thoughtlessness or to a dusty and ashen cynicism. Born potentially sane, he learns his madness. ' For every man,' as Sancho Pança remarked, ' is as heaven made him, and sometimes a great deal worse ' —sometimes, too, a great deal better ; it depends, partly on his own efforts, partly on the traditions, the beliefs, the codes, the philosophy of life that happen to be current in the society into which he was born. Where this social inheritance is a madness, the naturally sanest individual is moulded in the likeness of a madman. In relation to the society in which he lives he is of course sane ; for he resembles the majority of his fellows. But they are all, absolutely speaking, mad together.

Nature remains unaltered, whatever conscious efforts are made to distort her. Men may deny the existence of a part of their own spirit ; but what is denied is not thereby destroyed. The outlawed elements take their revenge on individuals, on whole societies. One thing alone is absolutely certain of the future : that our Western societies will not long persist in their present state. Mad ideals and a lunatic philosophy of life are not the best guarantees of survival.

A NOTE ON EUGENICS

THE SICK PHILOSOPHER

When the microcosm is sick, the macrocosm is liable to be infected with its diseases. A bilious philosopher's opinion of the world can only be accepted with a pinch of salt, of Epsom salt by preference. When we have discounted his pains and antidoted his dyspeptic self-poisoning, his philosophy generally assumes a new aspect. Leopardi was one of those sick unhappy thinkers who inoculate the universe with their own maladies. Himself half blind and hard of hearing, he put out the eyes of the world and made it deaf to the cries of man. Suffering, he filled the world with his own pain. Most of the bitter and gloomy things he said about the cosmos were really said about himself. Most, but not all. There are some whose truth even a man in health must admit. The words that follow, for example, are not the comment of a sick man on his own malady. They are the statement of mere unpleasant facts.

'The human race,' he writes, ' is divided into two parts : some use oppressive power, others suffer it. Since neither law nor any force, nor progress of philosophy or civilization can prevent any man born or yet to be born from

272

belonging to one or other party, it remains for him who can choose to choose. Not all, it is true, can choose, nor at all times.'

That these words are true of the past and present is sufficiently obvious. There have always been, there still are, a few oppressors and many oppressed—in the mildest and most auspicious circumstances a few more or less tyrannous rulers and many ruled. With regard to the future, who dares to be certain ? The best a prophet can do is to search the past and the present for sets of constantly recurring correlations and trust in the order of the universe. If human nature persists in its present form and the same causes go on producing the same effects, then we can feel fairly safe in believing with Leopardi that no amount of law or civilization can essentially change the relations between the two classes of men. If the majority of human beings continue to be born dull-witted, with a dread of thought and responsibility, it is obvious that they will continue to be dominated by the strong, intelligent, and active minority. The only event that can falsify Leopardi's prophecy is a change in individual human nature, or a change in the character of society as a whole, brought about by change in the relative numbers of the constituent types. The first contingency may safely be neglected. It is almost infinitely improbable that from a given date onwards all babies will be born lacking, shall we say, the sexual instinct, but gifted with infallible intuition. And even if such a thing were likely to happen, it would be quite impossible for us who have a sexual instinct and very inadequate intuition to imagine what its results would be. Inability to talk about a thing is an excellent reason for preserving silence. Unfortunately, however, it is not a reason that is apparent to every one. Human history reverberates with the noisy discussion of the undiscussable. I will refrain from increasing the quite unnecessary uproar.

SOCIAL DEGENERATION

The second of our contingencies is the more interesting, because it may quite conceivably be realized ; and since it involves no radical change or innovation, but only a rearrangement of existing and well-known elements, it is possible for us to give a reasonable forecast of its results. The constitution of society may change in two ways. Either the numbers of the inferior types may increase at the expense of the superior, or the numbers of the superior at the expense of the inferior. The eugenists assure us that the first of these alternatives is actually being realized, and advise us to take steps to reverse the process. The causes of social degeneration —which means the multiplication of inferior types at the expense of the superior—have often been described. It is unnecessary for me to give more than the briefest summary of them here. The first is that physically and mentally defective individuals are now preserved in greater quantities than at any other period. Humanitarianism has provided the incentive, political security and medical science the means, for achieving this preservation of those whom nature would regard as unfit to survive. And deficients are not only preserved : they are also permitted to multiply their kind. There is evidence to show that they are more than ordinarily fertile. The second cause of deterioration is to be found in the differential multiplication of the social classes. In most countries the birth-rate in the professional and artisan class is much lower than that among unskilled and casual labourers. There are apparently various reasons for this state of things, into which, however, it is unnecessary to go here. It is enough for our purposes to know that the classes do increase at different rates. Now, if it can be shown—as it can—that the average ability of the unskilled or casual worker is lower than the average ability of the skilled and professional worker, then it is obvious that, given differences in the rate of multiplication, the inferior types are being increased at the expense of the superior types. Moreover, superior individuals who rise from lower to higher social levels do not as a rule carry with them the habits of fertility common in the ranks from which they have risen, but tend to acquire the habits of birth-control current in the class in which they have made their way. That is to say that (whatever the reasons may be) superior individuals tend to be sterilized in proportion as they succeed. The eugenists are alarmed by this state of affairs, and have proposed various remedies, some practical and some fantastically Utopian.

They range from modest proposals to sterilize the mentally deficient and reward with bonuses the fertility of the intelligent, to the wildest schemes for making stallions of men of genius and forbidding ordinary human beings to have any children at all. None of these schemes requires discussion here. In the present essay I am not concerned to argue for or against eugenic reform. I merely ask myself a question : what would be the effects on society of considerable deterioration on the one hand, or considerable eugenic improvement on the other? and propose some speculative answers. Let us begin with deterioration. It is obvious that if a deteriorating society is surrounded by flourishing neighbours it will be overrun by its stronger rivals. Conquest, if it is accompanied by military slaughter, economic ruin and consequent starvation, and the interbreeding of the survivors with superior invaders, may result in the regeneration of the deteriorated society.

The case of Rome is perhaps a valid example. Where the deteriorating society is isolated, or surrounded by neighbours among whom the multiplication of inferior at the expense of superior types is going on at the same rate, such dramatic catastrophes are not to be expected. The first results of deterioration will be to put an exceptionally high premium on superiority. In a society where the inferior elements are on the increase, the few superior men will have an unusually good chance to acquire power and influence. It will be an age of sub-men and super-men. If the degeneration is allowed to continue unchecked, the breed of superior men will be altogether eliminated ; and the process is likely to be hastened by a revolt of the numerically powerful sub-men. In societies like our own the inferior are in a very strong position, because they are technically trained. If he has a gun and can shoot straight, a chimpanzee is a match for Napoleon. When the masses of the coloured races are as well trained and highly industrialized as our own, we shall have little or nothing on our side to outweigh their numbers. Twenty years ago Mr. Belloc could write the memorable lines,

> Whatever happens, we have got
> The Maxim gun and they have not.

This statement is already not as true as it was, and in a few generations will be only too distressingly false. The white races will be at the mercy of the coloured races, and the superior whites will be at the mercy of their white inferiors.

EUGENIC REFORM

It is not likely, however, that men will allow the process of deterioration to go to such dangerous lengths. The reaction to manifest deterioration will be a policy of eugenics. What methods the eugenists will employ to improve the stock I shall not try to guess. It is quite possible, as Mr. J. B. S. Haldane has suggested, that biological technique will soon have advanced to such a pitch that scientists will succeed in doing what Dr. Erasmus Darwin and Miss Anna Seward, the Swan of Lichfield, tried, it is said, and failed to do : they will learn to breed babies in bottles. If this should become feasible, then every genius will be able, like David in the poem, to ' scatter his Maker's image through the land.' But whatever means of racial improvement are adapted, I take it that the criterion of human excellence, and with it the eugenic goal, will remain more or less the same. In his book, *The Need of Eugenic Reform*, Major Leonard Darwin admits that, except in those extreme cases where abnormally gifted or abnormally deficient individuals are concerned, we have no precisely formulated standard of eugenic fitness. To sterilize the manifestly

278

deficient and encourage the fertility of the manifestly superior individual is a comparatively easy task ; but the results would be negligible, because the great mass of the population would remain unaffected. Major Darwin finds that in a society organized on contemporary lines there is a correlation between eugenic fitness and wage-earning capacity. We regard as desirable the qualities that make for social success ; these qualities must therefore be fostered. Major Darwin has elaborated a scheme for the systematic discouragement of fertility among the ill-paid and its encouragement among the well-paid. I need not go into the details here. If practical politicians accept Major Darwin's substitute for a standard of eugenic fitness—and it is difficult to see what other they can find—we shall have a society compelled by law to breed more and more exclusively from its most gifted and socially most successful members. What will be the results ?

PROBABLE EFFECTS OF EUGENIC REFORM

In India, where there are very few openings for educated men, the products of university training are a drug on the market. You can hire a Brahman Master of Arts to be your secretary more cheaply than you can hire some low-caste fellow, whose mere proximity would defile the other man, to be your cook. The educated unemployed of India feel, not unnaturally, as though they had been cheated out of their rights. Their discontent, as generally happens in these cases, is turned against the powers that be. They are the government's most dangerous enemies, or would be if Indians were ever the dangerous enemies of any one but themselves. States in which eugenic reform has multiplied the number of superior individuals at the expense of their inferiors will be like the India of to-day ; but with this difference, that while the unemployed and misemployed malcontents of India are only men who happen to have gone through an inadequate university training, the malcontents of the eugenic state will be people of real ability, conscious of their powers and indignant at not being permitted to use them. For it is obvious that all the superior individuals of the eugenic state will not be permitted to make full use of their powers, for the good reason that no society provides openings for more than a limited number of superior people. Not more than a few men can govern, do scientific research, practise the arts, hold responsible positions, or lead their fellows. There must be subjects as well as rulers, farmers as well as mathematical physicists, bank clerks as well as poets, workmen as well as managers, private soldiers as well as officers. But if, as would be the case

in a perfectly eugenized state, every individual
is capable of playing the superior part, who
will consent or be content to do the dirty
work and obey? The inhabitants of one of
Mr. Wells's numerous Utopias solve the problem
by ruling and being ruled, doing high-brow and
low-brow work, in turns. While Jones plays
the piano, Smith spreads the manure. At the
end of the shift they change places; Jones
trudges out to the dung-heap and Smith prac-
tises the A minor Etude of Chopin. An admirable state of affairs if it could be arranged. But
looking at the socially successful and gifted men
of to-day, can we believe that their descendants
will ever possess the sweet reasonableness and
mutual forbearance required in those who
would make such an arrangement? Personally,
I find my faith too weak. A population of men
and women descended mainly or exclusively
from the successful politicians, professional men,
and industrialists, from the most highly gifted
artists, mathematicians, and men of science,
from the most ravishing cabaret actresses and
the most efficient female M.P.'s and lady doctors
of the preceding generation, would live in a
state, so far as I can see, of chronic civil war.
Strength of will, determination, obstinacy, and
ambition are among the chief ingredients of
the socially successful individual. The intellectually gifted are notorious for the ruthless way
in which they cultivate their gifts, regardless

of what the rest of the world may think or
desire. Their children are just as likely to
inherit these characteristics from their parents
as they are to inherit their intelligence or the
shape of their noses. States function as smoothly
as they do, because the greater part of the
population is not very intelligent, dreads responsibility, and desires nothing better than to be
told what to do. Provided the rulers do not
interfere with its material comforts and its
cherished beliefs, it is perfectly happy to let
itself be ruled. The socially efficient and the
intellectually gifted are precisely those who
are not content to be ruled, but are ambitious
either to rule or to live in an anti-social solitude.
A state with a population consisting of nothing
but these superior people could not hope to
last for a year. The best is ever the enemy of
the good. If the eugenists are in too much
of an enthusiastic hurry to improve the race,
they will only succeed in destroying it.

COMFORT

NOVELTY OF THE PHENOMENON

French hotel-keepers call it *Le confort moderne*, and they are right. For comfort is a thing of recent growth, younger than steam, a child when telegraphy was born, only a generation older than radio. The invention of the means of being comfortable and the pursuit of comfort as a desirable end—one of the most desirable that human beings can propose to themselves—are modern phenomena, unparalleled in history since the time of the Romans. Like all phenomena with which we are extremely familiar, we take them for granted, as a fish takes the water in which it lives, not realizing the oddity and novelty of them, not bothering to consider their significance. The padded chair, the well-sprung bed, the sofa, central heating, and the regular hot bath—these and a host of other comforts enter into the daily lives of even the most moderately prosperous of the Anglo-Saxon bourgeoisie. Three hundred years ago they were unknown to the greatest kings. This is a curious fact which deserves to be examined and analysed.

The first thing that strikes one about the discomfort in which our ancestors lived is that it was mainly voluntary. Some of the apparatus of modern comfort is of purely modern invention ; people could not put rubber tyres on their carriages before the discovery of South America and the rubber plant. But for the most part there is nothing new about the material basis of our comfort. Men could have made sofas and smoking - room chairs, could have installed bathrooms and central heating and sanitary plumbing any time during the last three or four thousand years. And as a matter of fact, at certain periods they did indulge themselves in these comforts. Two thousand years before Christ, the inhabitants of Cnossos were familiar with sanitary plumbing. The Romans had invented an elaborate system of hot-air heating, and the bathing facilities in a smart Roman villa were luxurious and complete beyond the dreams of the modern man. There were sweating - rooms, massage - rooms, cold plunges, tepid drying - rooms with (if we may believe Sidonius Apollinaris) improper frescoes on the walls and comfortable couches where you could lie and get dry and talk to your friends. As for the public baths they were almost inconceivably luxurious. ' To such a height of luxury have we reached,' said Seneca, ' that we are dissatisfied if, in our baths, we do not tread on gems.' The size and completeness of the thermae was proportionable to their splendour. A single room of the baths of Diocletian has been transformed into a large church.

It would be possible to adduce many other examples showing what could be done with the limited means at our ancestors' disposal in the way of making life comfortable. They show sufficiently clearly that if the men of the Middle Ages and early modern epoch lived in filth and discomfort, it was not for any lack or ability to change their mode of life ; it was because they chose to live in this way, because filth and discomfort fitted in with their principles and prejudices, political, moral, and religious.

COMFORT AND THE SPIRITUAL LIFE

What have comfort and cleanliness to do with politics, morals, and religion ? At a first glance one would say that there was and could be no causal connection between armchairs and democracies, sofas and the relaxation of the family system, hot baths and the decay of Christian orthodoxy. But look more closely and you will discover that there exists the closest connection between the recent growth of comfort and the recent history of ideas. I hope in this essay to make that connection manifest, to show why it was not possible (not materially, but psychologically impossible) for the Italian princes of the quattrocento, for the Elizabethan, even for Louis xiv. to live in what the Romans would have called common cleanliness and decency, or enjoy what would be to us indispensable comforts.

Let us begin with the consideration of arm-chairs and central heating. These, I propose to show, only became possible with the break-down of monarchical and feudal power and the decay of the old family and social hierarchies. Smoking - room chairs and sofas exist to be lolled in. In a well-made modern armchair you cannot do anything but loll. Now, lolling is neither dignified nor respectful. When we wish to appear impressive, when we have to administer a rebuke to an inferior, we do not lie in a deep chair with our feet on the mantel-piece ; we sit up and try to look majestical. Similarly, when we wish to be polite to a lady or show respect to the old or eminent, we cease to loll ; we stand, or at least we straighten our-selves up. Now, in the past human society was a hierarchy in which every man was always engaged in being impressive towards his in-feriors or respectful to those above him. Loll-ing in such societies was utterly impossible. It was as much out of the question for Louis xiv. to loll in the presence of his courtiers as it was for them to loll in the presence of their king. It was only when he attended a session of the Parlement that the King of France ever lolled in public. On these occasions he reclined in the Bed of Justice, while princes sat, the great officers of the crown stood, and the smaller fry knelt. Comfort was proclaimed as the appanage of royalty. Only the king might stretch his legs. We may feel sure, however, that he stretched them in a very majestic manner. The lolling was purely ceremonial and accompanied by no loss of dignity. At ordinary times the king was seated, it is true, but seated in a dignified and upright position ; the appearance of majesty had to be kept up. (For, after all, majesty is mainly a question of majestical appearance.) The courtiers, meanwhile, kept up the appearances of deference, either standing, or else, if their rank was very high and their blood peculiarly blue, sitting, even in the royal presence, on stools. What was true of the king's court was true of the nobleman's household ; and the squire was to his dependants, the merchant was to his apprentices and servants, what the monarch was to his courtiers. In all cases the superior had to express his superiority by being dignified, the inferior his inferiority by being deferential ; there could be no lolling. Even in the intimacies of family life it was the same : the parents ruled like popes and princes, by divine right ; the children were their subjects. Our fathers took the fifth commandment very seriously—how seriously may be judged from the fact that during the great Calvin's theocratic rule of Geneva a child was publicly decapitated for having ventured to strike its parents. Lolling on the part of children, though not perhaps a capital offence, would have been regarded as an act of the grossest disrespect, punishable by much flagellation, starving, and confinement. For a slighter insult — neglect to touch his cap — Vespasiano Gonzaga kicked his only son to death ; one shudders to think what he might have been provoked to do if the boy had lolled. If the children might not loll in the presence of their parents, neither might the parents loll in the presence of their children, for fear of demeaning themselves in the eyes of those whose duty it was to honour them. Thus we see that in the European society of two or three hundred years ago it was impossible for any one—from the Holy Roman Emperor and the King of France down to the poorest beggar, from the bearded patriarch to the baby—to loll in the presence of any one else. Old furniture reflects the physical habits of the hierarchical society for which it was made. It was in the power of mediaeval and renaissance craftsmen to create armchairs and sofas that might have rivalled in comfort those of to-day. But society being what, in fact, it was, they did nothing of the kind. It was not, indeed, until the sixteenth century that chairs became at all common. Before that time a chair was a symbol of authority. Committee-men now loll, Members of Parliament are comfortably seated, but authority still belongs to a Chairman, still issues from a symbolical Chair. In the Middle Ages only the great had chairs. When a great man travelled, he took his chair with him, so that he might never be seen detached from the outward and visible sign of his authority. To this day the Throne no less than the Crown is the symbol of royalty. In mediaeval times the vulgar sat, whenever it was permissible for them to sit, on benches, stools, and settles. With the rise, during the Renaissance period, of a rich and independent bourgeoisie, chairs began to be more freely used. Those who could afford chairs sat in them, but sat with dignity and discomfort ; for the chairs of the sixteenth century were still very throne-like, and imposed upon those who sat in them a painfully majestic attitude. It was only in the eighteenth century, when the old hierarchies were seriously breaking up, that furniture began to be comfortable. And even then there was no real lolling. Armchairs and sofas on which men (and, later, women) might indecorously sprawl, were not made until democracy was firmly established, the middle classes enlarged to gigantic proportions, good manners lost from out of the world, women emancipated, and family restraints dissolved.

CENTRAL HEATING AND THE FEUDAL SYSTEM

Another essential component of modern comfort—the adequate heating of houses—was made impossible, at least for the great ones of the earth, by the political structure of ancient societies. Plebeians were more fortunate in this respect than nobles. Living in small houses, they were able to keep warm. But the nobleman, the prince, the king, and the cardinal inhabited palaces of a grandeur corresponding with their social position. In order to prove that they were greater than other men, they had to live in surroundings considerably more than life-size. They received their guests in vast halls like roller-skating rinks; they marched in solemn processions along galleries as long and as draughty as Alpine tunnels, up and down triumphal staircases that looked like the cataracts of the Nile frozen into marble. Being what he was, a great man in those days had to spend a great deal of his time in performing solemn symbolical charades and pompous ballets—performances which required a lot of room to accommodate the numerous actors and spectators. This explains the enormous dimensions of royal and princely palaces, even of the houses of ordinary landed gentlemen. They owed it to their position to live, as though they were giants, in rooms a hundred feet long and thirty high. How splendid, how magnificent! But oh, how bleak! In our days the self-made great are not expected to keep up their position in the splendid style of those who were great by divine right.

Sacrificing grandiosity to comfort, they live in rooms small enough to be heated. (And so, when they were off duty, did the great in the past ; most old palaces contain a series of tiny apartments to which their owners retired when the charades of state were over. But the charades were long - drawn affairs, and the unhappy princes of old days had to spend a great deal of time being magnificent in icy audience-chambers and among the whistling draughts of interminable galleries.) Driving in the environs of Chicago, I was shown the house of a man who was reputed to be one of the richest and most influential of the city. It was a medium-sized house of perhaps fifteen or twenty smallish rooms. I looked at it in astonishment, thinking of the vast palaces in which I myself have lived in Italy (for considerably less rent than one would have to pay for garaging a Ford in Chicago). I remembered the rows of bedrooms as big as ordinary ballrooms, the drawing-rooms like railway stations, the staircase on which you could drive a couple of limousines abreast. Noble *palazzi*, where one has room to feel oneself a superman ! But remembering also those terrible winds that blow in February from the Apennines, I was inclined to think that the rich man of Chicago had done well in sacrificing the magnificences on which his counterpart in another age and country would have spent his riches.

PROPER STUDIES

BATHS AND MORALS

It is to the decay of monarchy, aristocracy, and ancient social hierarchy that we owe the two components of modern comfort hitherto discussed ; the third great component—the bath—must, I think, be attributed, at any rate in part, to the decay of Christian morals. There are still on the continent of Europe, and for all I know, elsewhere, convent schools in which young ladies are brought up to believe that human bodies are objects of so impure and obscene a character that it is sinful for them to see, not merely other people's nakedness, but even their own. Baths, when they are permitted to take them (every alternate Saturday) must be taken in a chemise descending well below the knees. And they are even taught a special technique of dressing which guarantees them from catching so much as a glimpse of their own skin. These schools are now, happily, exceptional, but there was a time, not so long ago, when they were the rule. Theirs is the great Christian ascetic tradition which has flowed on in majestic continuity from the time of St. Anthony and the unwashed, underfed, sex-starved monks of the Thebaid, through the centuries, almost to the present day. It is to the weakening of that tradition that women at any rate owe the luxury of frequent bathing.

The early Christians were by no means

enthusiastic bathers ; but it is fair to point out that Christian ascetic tradition has not at all times been hostile to baths as such. That the Early Fathers should have found the promiscuity of Roman bathing shocking is only natural. But the more moderate of them were prepared to allow a limited amount of washing, provided that the business was done with decency. The final decay of the great Roman baths was as much due to the destructiveness of the Barbarians as to Christian ascetic objections. During the Ages of Faith there was actually a revival of bathing. The Crusaders came back from the East, bringing with them the oriental vapour bath, which seems to have had a considerable popularity all over Europe. For reasons which it is difficult to understand, its popularity gradually waned, and the men and women of the late sixteenth and early seventeenth centuries seem to have been almost as dirty as their barbarous ancestors. Medical theory and court fashions may have had something to do with these fluctuations.

The ascetic tradition was always strongest where women were concerned. The Goncourts record in their diary the opinion, which seems to have been current in respectable circles during the Second Empire, that female immodesty and immorality had increased with the growth of the bath habit. ' Girls should wash less,' was the obvious corollary. Young ladies who enjoy their bath owe a debt of gratitude to Voltaire for his mockeries, to the nineteenth-century scientists for their materialism. If these men had never lived to undermine the convent school tradition, our girls might still be as modest and as dirty as their ancestresses.

COMFORT AND MEDICINE

It is, however, to the doctors that bath-lovers owe their greatest debt. The discovery of microbic infection has put a premium on cleanliness. We wash now with religious fervour, like the Hindus. Our baths have become something like magic rites to protect us from the powers of evil, embodied in the dirt-loving germ. We may venture to prophesy that this medical religion will go still further in undermining the Christian ascetic tradition. Since the discovery of the beneficial effects of sunlight, too much clothing has become, medically speaking, a sin. Immodesty is now a virtue. It is quite likely that the doctors, whose prestige among us is almost equal to that of the medicine men among their savages, will have us stark naked before very long. That will be the last stage in the process of making clothes more comfortable. It is a process which has been going on for some time—first among men, later among women—and among its determining causes are the decay of hierarchic formalism and of Christian morality. In his lively little pamphlet describing Gladstone's visit to Oxford shortly before his death, Mr. Fletcher has recorded the Grand Old Man's comments on the dress of the undergraduates. Mr. Gladstone, it appears, was distressed by the informality and the cheapness of the students' clothes. In his day, he said, young men went about with a hundred pounds worth of clothes and jewellery on their persons, and every self-respecting youth had at least one pair of trousers in which he never sat down for fear of spoiling its shape. Mr. Gladstone visited Oxford at a time when undergraduates still wore very high starched collars and bowler hats. One wonders what he would have said of the open shirts, the gaudily coloured sweaters, the loose flannel trousers of the present generation. Dignified appearances have never been less assiduously kept up than they are at present ; informality has reached an unprecedented pitch. On all but the most solemn occasions a man, whatever his rank or position, may wear what he finds comfortable.

The obstacles in the way of women's comforts were moral as well as political. Women were compelled not merely to keep up social appearances, but also to conform to a tradition of Christian ascetic morality. Long after men had abandoned their uncomfortable formal clothes, women were still submitting to extraordinary inconveniences in the name of modesty.

It was the war which liberated them from their bondage. When women began to do war work, they found that the traditional modesty in dress was not compatible with efficiency. They preferred to be efficient. Having discovered the advantages of immodesty, they have remained immodest ever since, to the great improvement of their health and increase of their personal comfort. Modern fashions are the most comfortable that women have ever worn. Even the ancient Greeks were probably less comfortable. Their under-tunic, it is true, was as rational a garment as you could wish for ; but their outer robe was simply a piece of stuff wound round the body like an Indian *sari*, and fastened with safety-pins. No woman whose appearance depended on safety-pins can ever have felt really comfortable.

COMFORT AS AN END IN ITSELF

Made possible by changes in the traditional philosophy of life, comfort is now one of the causes of its own further spread. For comfort has now become a physical habit, a fashion, an ideal to be pursued for its own sake. The more comfort is brought into the world, the more it is likely to be valued. To those who have known comfort, discomfort is a real torture. And the fashion which now decrees the worship of comfort is quite as imperious as any other fashion. Moreover, enormous material interests are bound up with the supply of the means of comfort. The manfacturers of furniture, of heating apparatus, of plumbing fixtures, cannot afford to let the love of comfort die. In modern advertisement they have means for compelling it to live and grow.

Having now briefly traced the spiritual origins of modern comfort, I must say a few words about its effects. One can never have something for nothing, and the achievement of comfort has been accompanied by a compensating loss of other equally, or perhaps more, valuable things. A man of means who builds a house to-day is in general concerned primarily with the comfort of his future residence. He will spend a great deal of money (for comfort is very expensive : in America they talk of giving away the house with the plumbing) on bathrooms, heating apparatus, padded furnishings, and the like ; and having spent it, he will regard his house as perfect. His counterpart in an earlier age would have been primarily concerned with the impressiveness and magnificence of his dwelling—with beauty, in a word, rather than comfort. The money our contemporary would spend on baths and central heating would have been spent in the past on marble staircases, a grand façade, frescoes, huge suites of gilded rooms, pictures, statues. Sixteenth-century popes lived in a discomfort that a modern bank manager would consider unbearable ; but they had Raphael's frescoes, they had the Sistine chapel, they had their galleries of ancient sculpture. Must we pity them for the absence from the Vatican of bathrooms, central heating, and smoking-room chairs? I am inclined to think that our present passion for comfort is a little exaggerated. Though I personally enjoy comfort, I have lived very happily in houses devoid of almost everything that Anglo-Saxons deem indispensable. Orientals and even South Europeans, who know not comfort and live very much as our ancestors lived centuries ago, seem to get on very well without our elaborate and costly apparatus of padded luxury. I am old-fashioned enough to believe in higher and lower things, and can see no point in material progress except in so far as it subserves thought. I like labour-saving devices, because they economize time and energy which may be devoted to mental labour. (But then I enjoy mental labour ; there are plenty of people who detest it, and who feel as much enthusiasm for thought-saving devices as for automatic dishwashers and sewing-machines.) I like rapid and easy transport, because by enlarging the world in which men can live it enlarges their minds. Comfort for me has a similar justification : it facilitates mental life. Discomfort handicaps thought ; it is difficult when the body is cold and aching to use the